Victorian Women Travel Writers in Africa

Twayne's English Authors Series

Herbert Sussman, Editor

Northeastern University

TEAS 349

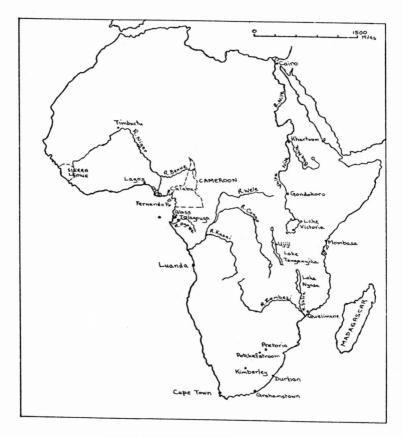

AFRICA IN THE NINETEENTH CENTURY

Victorian Women Travel Writers in Africa

By Catherine Barnes Stevenson

University of Hartford

Twayne Publishers • *Boston*

Victorian Women Travel Writers in Africa

Catherine Barnes Stevenson

Copyright © 1982 by G. K. Hall & Company
All Rights Reserved
Published by Twayne Publishers
A Division of G. K. Hall & Company
70 Lincoln Street
Boston, Massachusetts 02111

Book Production by Marne B. Sultz
Book Design by Barbara Anderson

Printed on permanent/durable acid-free
paper and bound in The United States
of America.

Library of Congress Cataloging in Publication Data

Stevenson, Catherine Barnes.
  Victorian women travel writers in Africa.

  (Twayne's English authors series ; TEAS 349)
  Bibliography: p. 176
  Includes index.
    1. English prose literature—19th century—History
and criticism.   2. English prose literature—Women
authors—History and criticism.   3. Travelers, Women—
Africa—Biography.   4. British—Africa—Biography.
5. Africa—History—19th century.   I. Title.   II. Series.
PR788.T72S8 1982   828'.808'099287   82–11851
ISBN 0–8057–6835–1

Contents

About the Author

Catherine Barnes Stevenson is an assistant professor of English at the University of Hartford, Connecticut. She received the B.A. from Manhattanville College and the M.A. and Ph.D. in English Literature from New York University. The recipient of fellowships from the Woodrow Wilson and Danforth Foundations, she has also been awarded two National Endowment for the Humanities grants and the University of Hartford's Vincent B. Coffin Award. Her teaching interests include Victorian poetry and women writers of the nineteenth and twentieth centuries, and she has published several articles on the poetry of Tennyson, as well as on Philip Sidney, Sarah Orne Jewett, Emily Tennyson, and Mary Kingsley. One of the founding editors of the *Victorian Studies Bulletin,* she has been its editor-in-chief since 1979.

Preface

In the eighteenth and nineteenth centuries an ever-increasing number of British women travelled to distant lands and recorded their experiences in print for an audience that eagerly read travel books. The narratives they produced offer fascinating glimpses not only of the lands to which these women travelled but also of the lives and self-perceptions of the travellers themselves. They are, thus, documents in the history and literature of travel, in British history, and in women's history; they are documents that have never before been accorded a comprehensive or scholarly study. Since a survey of all travel writing by British women would encompass volumes, this book focuses only on travel during one time period—the years of Queen Victoria's reign, 1837–1901—and to one continent, Africa.

During Victoria's reign Africa was transformed from a "dark" continent, a mythical place about which few Britons knew anything substantive, into a land whose hidden depths had been explored by popular heroes like David Livingstone, Samuel W. Baker, Henry M. Stanley, and Richard Burton; a land where British missionaries had spread the word of Christianity to remote villages and where British philanthropists had waged a war against the inhumane slave trade; a land increasingly populated by British soldiers, adventurers, traders, travellers, and settlers. During the sixty-three years under consideration, Britain's political involvement in Africa escalated as well. Initially reluctant to establish an African empire and to commit money and troops to maintaining control over lands where the British had settled, the government nonetheless found itself entangled in a series of wars with African tribes (the "Kaffir Wars," 1811–1879; the Zulu War, 1879; the "Gun War," 1878–1880; the Ashanti War, 1873; the Hut Tax Rebellion, 1898) and with Dutch settlers in South Africa (the two Anglo-Boer Wars, 1880–1881 and 1899–1900).

VICTORIAN WOMEN TRAVEL WRITERS IN AFRICA

By the 1880s the "scramble" for African territory had begun among the European powers, and Britain's imperial mission was extended to include the once-neglected Africa.

Against this historical backdrop, chapter 1 examines the forces that impelled nineteenth-century women, idealized by their culture as "angels in the house," to leave not only their houses but their native land to journey to Africa. It proposes a grouping of Victorian women travellers according to their motives for travel: wifely duty, missionary zeal, the search for adventure or escape, and professional interests. Such categorization in turn makes it possible to identify recurring themes or literary techniques that are common to the books produced by certain kinds of travellers. The literary characteristics of travel writing—that mixed genre which combines autobiography, historical narrative, scientific prose, dramatic scene painting, and political propaganda—are also discussed in the first chapter. As the *Cambridge History of English Literature* rightly observes, travel writers "are remembered as travellers rather than as authors and the value of their work lies not so much in revealing the personality and literary power of the writer as in successfully describing his journeys and discoveries."[1] Because of the difficulty of critically analyzing such writing, chapter 1 proposes several flexible, catholic criteria which can be used to assess the work of women travel writers: the clarity, accuracy, and vividness of their descriptions; the rhythmical and metaphorical power of their prose; the cultural objectivity, psychological complexity, and humor of their personae; and finally the "emplotment" of their travels into a cohesive story.

Chapters 2, 3, and 4 consider the actual writings of female travellers. Surveying a large body of writing by little-known wives, missionaries, and vacationers in Africa, chapter 2 identifies certain leitmotifs of this kind of travel writing: the hardships of African life, the domestic trials of a woman in Africa, the relationship between the female traveller and the Africans, and the woman's changing sense of self. In addition, it attempts to place each book in a historical, cultural, political, and literary context. Both chapters 3 and 4 then focus on a single woman traveller who merits extensive study because of her achievements as a traveller and as a writer. Both Florence Dixie and Mary Kingsley went to Africa for professional reasons, involved themselves in African politics, wrote lively, controversial travel narratives, and became public figures as a result. These chapters scrutinize the personal and social forces that shaped the personalities of these adventurous women, the journeys they undertook, and the psychological implications of these odysseys. Since both of these women were prolific authors, their travel writing is placed in the context of their other literary endeavors as well as in the cultural and political context of their time.

Catherine Barnes Stevenson

University of Hartford

Acknowledgments

I would like to thank the following for permission to quote: Department of Manuscripts, the British Library: Gladstone Papers and Macmillan Papers; Bodleian Library, Oxford University: Major Matthew Nathan Papers; National Library of Ireland: Stephen Gwynn Papers, Alice Stopford Green Papers, P. J. Smyth Papers; Royal Geographical Society: Mary Kingsley Papers; The Archives of the Council for World Mission: Hore Letters; the London School of Economics and Political Science: E. D. Morel Papers; John Holt and Co., Liverpool: Holt Papers.

Mrs. A. M. K. Covey-Crump for permission to quote from Mary Kingsley's writings.

Macmillan and Co., London, for passages from Stephen Gwynn's *The Life of Mary Kingsley*.

Frank Cass and Co., London, for passages from the third editions, revised, of *Travels in West Africa* and *West African Studies*.

I am deeply grateful to Penelope Lady Dixie for her generous hospitality and for permission to read private family papers. The enthusiastic encouragement of Mrs. Barbara Pontifex, Florence Dixie's granddaughter, greatly helped me, as did the family material she shared with me. Mrs. Dorothy Middleton, a pioneer in the study of women travellers, proved to be a magnanimous colleague who assisted me in locating Kingsley material. John Livingstone, Dan Stark, and George Michael Evica made valuable suggestions about my manuscript, for which I am deeply grateful.

Finally, I would like to thank the University of Hartford for the Vincent B. Coffin Grant and the Faculty Development Grant that made possible the preparation of this book. To my husband Keith, however, go the highest accolades for his patience, his good humor, and his suggestions to this modern woman traveller.

Chronology

1883   Kingsley family moves to Cambridge so that Mary's brother can attend university. Florence Dixie physically attacked at home in Windsor, March 17.

1884   Mrs. M. A. Pringle publishes *Towards the Mountains of the Moon*.

1886   Annie B. Hore publishes *To Lake Tanganyika in a Bath Chair*.

1889   Florence Dixie publishes the novels *Redeemed in Blood* and *The Young Castaways*.

1890   Florence Dixie publishes *Gloriana; or the Revolution of 1900* and *Aniwee; or the Warrior Queen: A Tale of the Araucanian Indians*.

1891   Jane Moir publishes *A Lady's Letters from Central Africa*. Florence Dixie publishes the pamphlet *The Horrors of Sport*.

1892   Mary Kingsley's parents die; she visits the Canary Islands.

1893   Mary Kingsley departs for West Africa in August. Fanny Barkly publishes *Among Boers and Basutos*.

1894   Mary Kingsley leaves for second trip to West Africa in December.

1895   Mary Kingsley returns home a celebrity in November. Alice Balfour publishes *Twelve Hundred Miles in a Waggon* about her 1884 journey through South Africa.

1897   Mary Kingsley publishes *Travels in West Africa*.

1899   Mary Kingsley publishes *West African Studies* and *The Story of West Africa*. Kingsley edits and publishes a collection of her father's writing, *Notes on Sport and Travel*. Anglo-Boer war begins.

1900   Mary Kingsley sails to South Africa to nurse Boer prisoners; dies there of enteric fever in June.

1901   First volume of Florence Dixie's *Songs of a Child and Other Poems by "Darling"* appears.

1902   Dixie publishes the second volume of *Songs of a Child* and *Isola; or the Disinherited* (written 1877).

1903   Florence Dixie publishes *The Story of Ijain, or the Evolution of a Mind.*

1905   Florence Dixie dies of diphtheria at Glen Stuart, Annan, November 7, leaving unfinished her novel *Izra, or a Child of Solitude.*

1906   *Izra* published as a book.

Chapter One
Women Travellers and the Art of Travel Writing

Background

Even before Victoria ascended the throne in 1837, a number of British women travellers had ventured to distant, exotic parts of the world and had recorded their various adventures. Margery Kempe, who visited Jerusalem and Rome in the fifteenth century, and left a record of this journey in her autobiography, *The Book of Margery Kempe* (1436), was followed in later centuries by several famous women. In 1716 Lady Mary Wortley Montagu accompanied her husband to Turkey, where she walked Constantinople's streets in native costume, visited a harem, and discovered the benefits of smallpox inoculation. Her vivid impressions and perceptive comments are preserved in *Letters Written during her Travels in Europe, Asia, and Africa* (1763). Lady Hester Stanhope, niece of Prime Minister William Pitt, left England in 1810 for a health-restoring journey to the Mediterranean; she never returned home but travelled throughout Turkey, Egypt, and the Middle East, visiting forbidden cities and eventually establishing herself in Lebanon as a kind of queen. In a less dramatic excursion, Mary Wollstonecraft, the famous feminist, journeyed alone with her infant daughter to Scandinavia on business for her lover Gilbert Imlay. Her perspicacious observations about the lifestyles, mores, and economics of the lands she visited, as well as her telling revelations about the difficulties faced by a woman travelling alone, are recorded in *Letters Written During a Short Residence in Sweden, Norway, and Denmark* (1796).

In the nineteenth century, because of the long peace after the Battle of Waterloo and the increasing prosperity of Britain, more and more women found themselves able to travel to Europe even without a male companion. With the increase in travel came an increased number of guidebooks, collections of travel hints, and diaries by travellers—many of which were written by or directed to women. But Europe could not long satisfy the adventurous Victorian woman traveller, so she sailed around the world (Lady Brassey), joined a French man-of-war in the South Seas (Constance Gordon-Cummings), rode across Arabia (Lady Anne Blunt), sailed up the Nile (Amelia Edwards and Lucie Duff Gordon), journeyed to America (Fanny Trollope and Harriet Martineau), and even ventured to remote corners of the Orient (Isabella Bird Bishop and Annie Taylor).[1] By the end of the century, handbooks for women travellers boldly asserted that "nowadays . . . a hundred women travel to one who ventured from the security of her roof tree in bygone days," and "there is in reality nothing to prevent a woman from seeing every civilized, and even semi-civilized, country in the world without other protection than her own modesty and good sense."[2] Armed with these virtues of the Victorian lady, women braved even the uncivilized wilds of Africa.

Although nineteenth-century women travelled for a variety of reasons, undoubtedly a major incentive was the desire to escape from domestic confinement and the social restrictions imposed on the Victorian female in Britain. As Dorothy Middleton observes, "Travel was an individual gesture of the house-bound, man-dominated Victorian woman."[3] The "caged birds" of the Victorian parlor found their wings and often took flight in other lands.[4] In a less constrained environment they achieved physical and psychological freedom and the illusion of autonomy. Davenport Adams in *Celebrated Women Travellers of the Nineteenth Century* (1883) comments: "Fettered as women are in highly civilized countries by restraints, obligations, and responsibilities, which are too often arbitrary and artificial . . . it is natural enough that when the opportunity offers, they should hail even a temporary emancipation through travel."[5] Lilias Campbell Davidson in *Hints to Lady Travellers At Home and Abroad* (1889) celebrates the "emancipation" of the woman traveller, who can be "her own unescorted and independent person."[6] And Paul Fussell has recently argued that a travel book is always "an implicit celebration of freedom."[7]

By the latter part of the nineteenth century, women travellers began to be singled out as exemplars of the new freedom and prowess of women. Journals like *Lady's Realm* and *Girls' Own Annual* featured series of articles on famous lady travellers which contended that "women can travel just as well as men if they only go to work in the right way."[8] Writing in *Blackwood's Magazine* (July 1896), W. C. Blaikie praised the accomplishments of women travellers "whose adventurous spirit has defied . . . hurricanes, shipwreck, arctic cold and darkness, and all other dangers and discomforts of the sea: and by land, fatigue, hunger, and sickness, robbers and extortioners, wild beasts, scorpions, mosquitoes, heat and cold, filth and fever, besides the nameless terrors of savage races, on whose whims they could not count, whose greed and ferocity shrank from no crime. In such an age as this we need wonder at nothing that women will dare."

Ironically, though many of these daring women opposed or were simply uninterested in the late Victorian campaigns to extend women's rights, they found that other people regarded their achievements as travellers as proof of female equality. Thus, Mary Kingsley returned from West Africa in 1895 to discover, with chagrin, that she was being hailed as a "new woman" because she was a daring traveller. By the end of the century, then, women's travel had taken on a political connotation. Even the traveller's choice of clothing was interpreted as a statement on women's role and position in contemporary society. To wear trousers, even in the jungle of Africa or the mountains of Tibet, was to identify oneself as an advocate of female emancipation. For example, the author of *Hints to Lady Travellers*, who approved of the liberating effect of travel, warned against "the modern feminine costume for mountaineering . . . where the skirt is a mere polite apology—an inch or two below the knee—and the result hardly consistent with a high ideal of womanhood."[9]

To reconcile that "high ideal of womanhood" with the new selves liberated by the experience of travel was a particular problem for women who ventured to primitive, perilous lands like Africa where they had occasion to act like men. Forced by circumstances to be hardy, courageous, and decisive, these women developed personae which, while still consciously ladylike, had a masculine authority and competence. The timid, dependent, nervous behavior expected of the woman at home had to be modified radically when she travelled. Thus, "The Art of Travel" (1894) recommends that lady travellers be "cool-headed, courteous, and self-reliant,"[10] and *Hints to Lady Travellers* notes that "courage and calmness in the hour of peril are no longer rare feminine virtues in the present day and even where they have not been bestowed by nature, they may very easily be acquired by cultivation and education."[11] In Africa women often had to assert their power physically in crisis situations. The American May French Sheldon, who travelled alone to Lake Chala, boasted that she flogged no more than ten men on her journey. She advised other women travellers to maintain discipline by physical chastisement of African guides and bearers and by setting a personal example of courage and discipline. Her own experience confirmed that when the Africans "found that I was always at the head of the caravan, and if there was any danger . . . they could rely on me, the result was that I soon obtained complete control over every man."[12]

Few women had Mrs. Sheldon's unqualified self-confidence or employed her firm methods, but many found themselves in the anomalous position of being "honorary men" in the eyes of Africans by virtue of their white skins. Still a rarity in most parts of Africa in the nineteenth century, women travellers were treated by indigenous peoples with a mixture of curiosity, reverence, and fear and were sometimes addressed as "Sir," "Mister," or, in May French Sheldon's case, "Bébé Bwana" (lady boss or "Mrs. Mister").[13] Clearly, they occupied a sexually ambiguous position. Granted the license to behave like men at moments when "typically" female conduct would have been not only ludicrous but dangerous, these women also were self-consciously female in appearance and behavior. Often they worried about how they were being perceived, what effect their unorthodox conduct or uncharacteristic appearance was having both on their travel companions and on their readers. In fact, Mary Wollstonecraft tartly observed that, when a woman goes on a journey, among her chief concerns are "the impression that she may make on her fellow-travellers; and . . . the care of her finery."[14]

Though self-conscious about their own femininity, women travellers did not, like their male counterparts, identify Africa as a female place—fecund, alluring, and dangerous.[15] Since most nineteenth-century women, excepting perhaps Florence Baker and Mary Kingsley, went to Africa as travellers rather than explorers, they did not seek to penetrate and to master the dark mysteries of an undiscovered land; instead, they attempted to combine "the excitement of the unpredictable attaching to exploration" with "the pleasure of 'knowing where one is.' "[16] Some female, like some male, travellers escaped from the confines of Britain to an Africa that promised adventure, personal freedom, or improved health. The journeys of other women travellers were motivated by their nation's political involvement on the African continent: a number of wives accompanied their husbands on official military or diplomatic missions in East, West, or South Africa. Others, fired by religious zeal, ventured into remote parts of the continent, alone or with families, to suppress the slave trade, convert and civilize Africans, and establish missions. Finally, a few women found professional reasons, like scientific research or journalism, to travel to Africa. Whatever their reasons for going, however, women travellers, like their male counterparts, took advantage of the popular vogue for travel writing by recording their experiences in books that are as much about themselves as about Africa.

The Form and Style of Travel Writing

The *Cambridge History of English Literature* attests to the enduring popularity of travel books which "have, probably, been more read in Great Britain than any other books except novels."[17] John Murray's advertisement for the "Home and Colonial library" suggests one reason for this popularity: "The aim of the publisher has been to produce a series of works as entertaining as romances, yet not frivolous, but abounding in sound information."[18] To a Victorian reader eager for "useful" information, a travel book offered hard facts about geography, history, botany, zoology, medicine, and ethnology; yet these data were couched in an often exciting narrative set in an exotic place and filled with terrifying adventures and strange people. Utilitarian or religious prejudices against imaginative literature did not extend to these accounts of real experience, even though they might contain material stranger and more titillating than any fictional creation. As Paul Fussell has observed, travel books are "romances in the old sense," set in actual landscapes and directed to "an audience which wants to go adventuring vicariously . . . but which at the same time wants to feel itself within a world declared real by such up-to-date studies as political science, sociology, anthropology, economics, and contemporary history."[19]

Travel narratives also appeal to readers by offering autobiographical and psychological insights: inward views of the traveller's responses to physical hardship, danger, emotional stress in an alien environment. During the nineteenth century, in fact, the personality of the traveller became an increasingly important facet of travel writing. Unlike eighteenth-century travel books, which convey "much leisurely information concerning monuments, customs and costumes; but . . . have about them little of the personal spirit, little of the lighter literary touch,"[20] Victorian travelogues tend to be more stylistically natural and lively, focusing less on the "sights" than on the relationship of men and women (including the traveller) to their environment. While enlightenment travellers wrote books of "pleasurable instruction" about foreign parts, their nineteenth-century counterparts often aimed to entertain readers with impressions of distant lands.[21] Indeed, the famous traveller to South America in the nineteenth century, Alexander von Humboldt, asserted that "it is the traveller himself whom we continually desire to see in contact with the objects which surround him."[22] That tradition of travel writing has carried through into the twentieth century; Norman

Douglas, reviewing Edward Doughty's *Arabia Deserta,* claimed that "an impersonal travel book is a horror" and that "the reader of a good travel book is entitled not only to an exterior voyage, to descriptions of scenery and so forth, but to an interior voyage, which takes place side by side with that outer one . . . the ideal book of this kind offers us, indeed, a triple opportunity of exploration—abroad, into the author's brain, and into your own."[23] In a number of instances, travel books by Victorian women do record, without overt psychologizing, that interior voyage, the "sea change in oneself that comes from immersion in another and savage culture."[24]

But, to record both the internal and external odysseys, a travel writer needs a style at once vividly descriptive, scientifically precise, and natural; moreover, he or she must create a narrative persona both convincingly reliable and engaging. In the eighteenth century a plain, unornamented style, combining both formal and colloquial language, was considered appropriate for travel writing.[25] Nineteenth-century critics of travel narratives also prized natural, unaffected prose that could maintain the illusion of immediacy in presenting both experience and emotion.[26] The creation of such a voice was essential to the construction of an attractive persona, one that could speak to the often diverse audiences of a travel narrative (the traveller's family, the general public, the scientific community, colonial office bureaucrats, etc.). John Tallmadge has demonstrated that Charles Darwin, in writing *The Voyage of the Beagle,* carefully shaped a persona capable of addressing his skeptical father, the scientific community, and the general public; in addition, he employed a number of rhetorical strategies to convince all three audiences of the "propriety, legitimacy, and worth"[27] of his five-year voyage to South America. Similarly, Mary Kingsley, in writing *Travels in West Africa* and *West African Studies,* tried to entertain and inform her three audiences—the public at large, the scientific community, and her friends on the West Coast of Africa. Attempting to speak to all of these groups in the same book, she developed a complex, schizophrenic narrative persona.

Not every traveller addresses such a wide audience; but all travel writers must select and arrange their experiences so as to create a comprehensible narrative. They must construct a "plot" for their adventures, observations, and feelings. T. D. MacLulich, analyzing the literature of Canadian exploration, has distinguished three ways in which travellers "emplot" their experiences: as quest-romances, as tragedies, and as odysseys. Explorers who are goal-oriented, who see their travels as conquests of a hostile environment accomplished by strength of will, write quest-romances. Those who are fired by the same goals but who fail in their quests write tragedies. On the other hand, those concerned not with the ends of their journey but with the experience of travel itself and with the lands they traverse write odysseys. In these narratives, "the incidental details of the journey become the main focal point of the account."[28]

Applying these distinctions to African travel narratives, it seems that male travellers are more likely to write quest-romances or tragedies while women are more likely to produce odysseys. For example, Samuel White Baker opens *The Albert N'yanza* by promising to take the reader by the hand, leading him along a rough and dangerous path "until I bring him, faint with the wearying journey, to that high cliff where the great prize shall burst upon his view—from which he shall look down upon the vast Albert Lake, and drink with me from the sources of the Nile!"[29] Likewise, Henry M. Stanley begins *Through the Dark Continent* by announcing that, after learning of David Livingstone's death, he was "fired" with a resolution to complete Livingstone's work, "to be, if God willed it, the next martyr to geographical science, or, if my life was to be spared, to clear up not only the secrets of the Great River [the Nile] throughout its course, but also all that remained still problematic and incomplete of the discoveries of Burton and Speke, and Speke and Grant."[30] Mary Kingsley, on the other hand, commences *Travels in West Africa* by confessing: "It was in 1893 that, for the first time in my life, I found myself in possession of five or six months which were not heavily forestalled, and feeling like a boy with a new half crown, I lay about in my mind . . . what to do with them.

'Go and learn your tropics,' said Science. . . . So I got down an atlas and saw that either South America or West Africa must be my destination."[31] Stanley and Baker clearly cast themselves in the heroic mold of the quester; Kingsley chooses the picaresque tradition. Stanley's travels are presented as the pursuit of an admirable object; Kingsley's as an unstructured, lighthearted search for new experiences. There are, of course, variations in the general pattern: David Livingstone's *Missionary Travels* (1857) presents his pioneering journey across Africa as an odyssey rather than a quest; conversely, Florence Dixie's *In the Land of Misfortune* (1882) begins with the quest motif but then depicts her actual travel experience as an odyssey.

That men and women regard the experience of travel differently was recognized as early as 1792 by Mary Wollstonecraft: "A man when he undertakes a journey, has in general, the end in view; a woman thinks more of the incidental occurrences, the strange things that may possibly occur on the road."[32] These contrary perceptions and modes of travel seem to express themselves in different kinds of narrative form. Women often cast their narratives as a series of letters home to a predominantly female audience interested in both the minutiae of everyday domestic life and the writer's psychological reactions to a new environment. The loose, accretive, epistolary form serves as an ideal vehicle for leisurely descriptions of diverse subjects—scenery, flora and fauna, housekeeping problems, food, politics, and local culture. Furthermore, the author of an epistolary travel account can easily slip from narrative to description, to personal rumination, to political commentary. But, even when they are not in letter form, women's travel narratives tend to be "generic hybrid[s] . . . subjective autobiography superimposed on a travelogue."[33] Because travel writing is a type of autobiographical narrative, recent studies of the differences between male and female autobiography provide a valuable perspective on the narrative structures chosen by travellers of the opposite sex. Men, these studies suggest, write formal, distilled autobiographies in which the primary concern is an objective evaluation of the significance of the whole life (or journey). Women, in contrast, produce more private, fragmented, episodic autobiographies (often in the form of a diary or series of letters) which impose no overarching design on their lives or travels.[34] Women tend to record, to surrender to experience; men to judge, to schematize experience.

The Content of Travel Writing

No matter what their sex or the structure of their narratives, all nineteenth-century travellers to Africa share a fascination with the geography and diverse peoples of the "dark continent." During that century European perceptions of Africans comprised a complex and shifting blend of mythology, ethnocentric prejudice, pseudoscience, and observation. Early in the century Africans were sometimes mythologized into noble savages living in an Arcadian world that was being destroyed by slavery.[35] As Victorian explorers encountered more Africans, however, a negative image gained popular acceptance. James Casada has observed "a pronounced tendency among the most noted explorers of Africa to dress up their travelogues with that which was sensational or outré or which served to call to notice the inferiority of the peoples among whom they travelled."[36] Samuel White Baker, for instance, depicted the African as "a creature of impulse, seldom actuated by reflection . . . callous and ungrateful" as well as a "cunning . . . liar."[37] The very notion of "the African," of course, testifies to a cultural bias which blinds the viewer to differences in tribal (not to mention in individual) character. Cultural bias was also evident in the exaggerated tales of African cannibalism which gained currency during the nineteenth century and which contributed to the conception of "the native" as a debased savage, a "connoisseur in cruelty."[38] Some Europeans compared African cruelty to that of thoughtless children, arguing that adult Africans were the mental equivalents of ten-year-old Europeans. When placed in a Darwinian frame of reference by certain commentators, such thinking produced assertions that African culture was on a lower rung in the evolutionary ladder than white European culture.[39] Consequently, it came to seem both inevitable and right that benevolent, paternalistic European powers would intervene in African affairs; would force Africans to adopt industry, thrift, and Christian morality; and would prevent them from regressing into savagery. From such premises arose the moral justification for nineteenth-century imperialism.

The attitudes of women travellers toward imperialism and toward Africans are not easily categorized. In general, however, most Victorian women travellers accept the notion of British superiority and sanction the presence of Britain in Africa. However, within this general framework of acceptance, they frequently voice strong criticism of their country's treatment of specific situations or particular African tribes. Often, women travellers display a special sympathy for and understanding of peoples whose skin color distinguishes them, as women often find themselves distinguished, as the "other," the alien. Even in situations where Africans are the enemy, women travellers, with the notable exception of Harriet Ward, seem reluctant to condemn or to cast racial slurs upon these adversaries. Some women even befriended reputedly ferocious African tribes: Florence Dixie identified herself with the Zulus while Mary Kingsley acknowledged a kinship with the cannibalistic Fans. These women also openly championed the cause of their adopted peoples, using their travel books as vehicles for political propaganda on the Africans' behalf.

Indeed, political argumentation of one sort or another is an important component in the writings of British women travellers to Africa. With varying degrees of reluctance, they advance firm opinions on Britain's conduct in Africa, reminding readers that such views are based on incontrovertible, empirical evidence. Women, who when at home were intellectually and experientially excluded from the world of politics, discovered themselves in Africa at the center of intense political activity. In addition, women in Africa were in a position to have unique knowledge about the political realities of African life, the cultural traditions of African peoples (known to those at home only through stereotyped or inaccurate descriptions), and the conditions at the war front during the various local skirmishes in which Britain engaged during Victoria's reign. Having personally experienced Africa, several women travellers eagerly added their voices to contemporary debates about British political involvement in African affairs, in some instances expressing trenchant criticism of their nation's imperialism.

In a number of ways, then, Africa altered the lives and self-perceptions of the women who travelled there. Their books provide intriguing three-dimensional portraits of their African adventures which reflect, first, the lands and peoples of the African continent as perceived by women; second, the large political drama of Britain's involvement in Africa in the nineteenth century; and, third, the inner psychological odysseys of women who, in acclimatizing themselves to alien cultures on remote continents, discovered new continents inside themselves.

Chapter Two

Wives, Missionaries, and Vacationers

Wives

Duty to husband, to family, or to God motivated most of the African travel by nineteenth-century British women. Like Richard Burton's wife, many heeded their husband's peremptory orders to "pay, pack, and follow" to remote parts of the world. They went, as a nineteenth-century commentator noted, "for the sake of the companionship of their husbands and possibly with a desire to see foreign lands."[1] This longing for adventure, a powerful but often tacit motive for female travel, is evident in the relish with which certain dutiful wives wrote about the dangers and hardships of their journeys.

Florence Baker and Katharine Petherick. One of the most famous and daring of these wifely travellers Florence Baker accompanied her husband, Samuel White Baker, on his 1862 explorations of the Nile tributaries and his 1870 expedition to Gondorko to suppress the slave trade. Praised by the President of the Royal Geographical Society as an example of "what a courageous wife can do in duty to her husband,"[2] Mrs. Baker acted with a calm decisiveness that saved her husband's life on at least one occasion. To readers in the nineteenth century, however, she was known only through her husband's travel books because her own journal and letters from Africa were not published until 1972.[3]

Marital duty drew another British wife into harrowing adventures in Africa. Katharine Petherick, wife of John Petherick, a mining engineer, trader, explorer, author, and British consul at

Khartoum, journeyed from England to Africa in 1861. After an exhilarating journey across the Nubian desert in which she revelled in the "charm" of her open-air "Bohemian life" (1:54),[4] Mrs. Petherick settled into a pleasant domestic routine at Khartoum. However, this life of ease did not last long. Her husband had been commissioned by the Royal Geographical Society to meet the famous explorers John Speke and James Grant at Gondorko and to resupply their expedition. Having left from Zanzibar in 1860, Speke and Grant had travelled to Lake Victoria, discovered the Nile's exit from the lake, and were to join the Pethericks in the summer of 1862. In March of that year Katharine and John Petherick, accompanied by a large party, began to ascend the Nile to Gondorko. Bad luck and inclement weather transformed the journey of a few months into a year-long odyssey which nearly claimed Mrs. Petherick's life. When they finally arrived at their destination in February 1863, four days after Speke and Grant, the Pethericks found themselves accused of duplicity—specifically, of stopping to trade ivory along the way rather than rushing to meet the expedition.

Feeling that his honor had been impugned by these accusations and deprived of his position as British consul as well as of his right to trade on the Nile, John Petherick left Egypt a disappointed and ill man. Thus, when Mr. and Mrs. Petherick wrote about their 1862–1863 journey in *Travels in Central Africa and Explorations of the Western Nile Tributaries* (1869), they emplotted their narrative as a tragedy, a failed quest which ended in defeat and departure from a hostile, nightmarish land. Their story is an apologia, a vindication of John Petherick's honesty and good intentions: the book's appendix, therefore, contains an extensive account of Petherick's agreement with the Royal Geographical Society, of the charges against him, and of his response.

But *Travels in Central Africa* also bears the mark of another, earlier narrative intent: Mrs. Petherick had planned to publish the journal of her Nile voyage with the Blackwood firm, but a severe attack of fever prevented the completion of the manuscript. The book that appeared in 1869 under both Pethericks' names employs Katharine Petherick's journal to supply the bulk of the narrative and her husband's diary to fill in scientific detail and narrate events that occurred when she was too ill to write. The narrative thus has the immediacy of action and emotion that diaries afford, but lacks a consistent tone, style, or perceptual framework since it comprises two separate narrative strands.

Mrs. Petherick's portion of *Travels in Central Africa* is colorful, emotional, and dramatic; it is narrated by a keen observer of people who can capture the emotional ambience of scenes in a few telling details. For example, a lavishly adorned and "magnificently formed young black woman" arrives on board their boat. After describing her clothing and jewelry in detail, Mrs. Petherick climaxes the physical description with a pointed psychological observation: "She tormented and made jealous her husband by talking and laughing with the soldiers and crew" (1:121). Similarly, the narrative persona powerfully re-creates the dramatic moment when a group of slaves is liberated from the hold of a boat: "And now from below stepped up one by one the discovered slaves (but slaves, thank God! no longer), giddy from excess of light, emerging from the dark hold, staggering . . . with outstretched hands. I received them—young girls and little children. . . . I had only tears" (1:138). Sympathetic to all Africans, but particularly to those victimized by slavery, she often dramatizes the agony of parents whose children have been stolen by slavers.

The warm, stalwart, adventurous woman who narrates part of *Travels* is reluctant—in the early part of the book at least—to dwell on the dangers or discomforts of travel. When she does admit to anguish or suffering, it is in a prose so direct and so devoid of self-pity that the heroic endurance of the persona is made all the more striking. Just before collapsing from fever, Mrs. Petherick records in her diary: "A wretched night . . . the roar of lions, and the firing occasionally at hyenas who come into the encampment quite unnerve me. Rain at noon, then hot sun: the mists then rising. I can see but a few paces before me—it is all so dismal" (1:196). The extent to which she understates her sufferings becomes clear in her husband's section of the narrative as he records her deliriums, her terrible sunburns, and her courageous endurance: "without a murmur as to her own serious discomfort . . . she had ever a cheering word to give our people" (1:219). He credits her "pluck" with inspiriting the group in moments of discouragement. Both narrations clearly indicate that Katharine Petherick is a strong yet always a traditionally feminine woman: compassionate, long-suffering, concerned about the impression that she is making on others. When they arrive at last at Gondorko, she gives few details about the celebrated explorers she meets there—Speke, Grant, and Baker—but does sketch her own distressing appearance: "Skin red-brown, face worn and haggard, hair scorched crisp, and clad in a scanty dress of gaudy calico, purchased from one of the soldiers" (1:312). Courageous, uncomplaining, totally committed to her husband's career, Mrs. Petherick, like Florence Baker, proved herself to be an invaluable companion, one who functioned well in the largely male world of African exploration. She also proved to be a vivid, unaffected narrator of harrowing experiences.

Few women whose wifely loyalty took them to Africa, however, had to abandon camp under hostile fire and march for days in enemy territory like Mrs. Baker or wander deliriously through the upper reaches of the Nile like Mrs. Petherick. In fact, a number of wives lead comparatively unadventurous, chiefly domestic, lives which they recorded in narratives filled with the details of their daily existence in Africa and their gradual psychological adjustment to this new, strange world. The universe limned in these narratives is almost exclusively a domestic, female one.

Elizabeth Melville.   An early travel narrative by an intrepid wife, Elizabeth Melville's *A Residence at Sierra Leone* (1849), focuses, by its author's own admission, on the "trivial matter" (v)[5] of daily life in a remote, unhealthy British colony on Africa's West Coast—a place where fewer than one hundred Europeans reside; where fierce hurricanes destroy part of the Melvilles' house, burying the family in rubble; and where fevers ravage Mrs. Melville, her husband, and her child. The author, who travelled to West Africa in 1840, is identified in the book's first edition simply as "a lady," in other words, a decorous, traditional, self-

effacing person. Indeed, Mrs. Melville maintains a ladylike silence
not only about her own name but about the names of other
Europeans in the colony, about her husband, and about their
reason for travelling to Sierra Leone, a place that came to be
known as "the white man's grave" because of its fatal climate.
Mrs. Melville admits that she omitted all potentially entertaining
"observations and anecdotes connected with European society of
the colony" (v) lest these bear too much resemblance to the reality.
A modern reader, of course, cannot help but wonder what slices
of colonial life ladylike discretion caused to be excised.

Given these omissions, what is the "trivial matter" on which
Mrs. Melville focuses? The exhausting attempt to manage a household under insupportable domestic conditions and to adjust psychologically to an inimical land—this is the heroism of which
Mrs. Melville and many women travellers write. For as Africa
provided a testing ground for masculine courage and strength of
will, it also afforded women the opportunity of proving their
valor. Some, like Florence Baker, Katharine Petherick, or Florence Dixie, demonstrated that one could be brave and hardy yet
still be feminine; others, who adopted the traditional female role
of housewife, proved the ingenuity, endurance, and mental stamina of the "ordinary" woman.

The housewife's burden, a common lament in books by wifely
travellers, is almost always accompanied by complaints about the
African as a servant. Thus, the indolence and unreliability of
Africans and the problems of finding and training servants are
leitmotifs of Mrs. Melville's narrative. But, despite her criticism
of Africans as servants, Mrs. Melville is not unsympathetic to the
plight of local blacks, many of whom have been recently liberated
from slavery and settled at Sierra Leone, a British colony since
1808 and a base for the antislavery compaign. With disarming
honesty, Mrs. Melville reflects on the stages through which Europeans pass in their response to Africans: their initial philanthropic impulses are soon countered by "despair" at the "indolence,
stupidity, and want of tidiness of the African" and can be diverted
into "a most sweeping kind of condemnation" of the whole race
(251). But sensitive, sympathetic Europeans move beyond this

attitude to question why West Coast Africans are this way. Mrs. Melville, having passed through these phases, adopts a surprisingly sympathetic attitude toward the causes of the behavior that Europeans find so frustrating: the Africans are as they are because of their oppression, first as slaves and then as residents of the British colony of Sierra Leone. And so, although she confesses to being "totally ignorant of most of the national usages and habits of the negroes" (226), Mrs. Melville displays a willingness to understand—and not to stereotype—the people among whom she lives.

Though not a student of African culture, Mrs. Melville is a passionate opponent of the slave trade. Like many women travellers, she modestly disclaims any political intent in her writing, yet she opens her narrative, by strongly defending Britain's efforts to end the traffic in slaves and by attacking those at home who would urge the abandonment of this noble venture which has been carried out "at the expense of so much British blood and treasure" (v). To emphasize her opposition to slavery she devotes chapters to discussing the capture and punishment of slave traders under international law; moreover, she dramatizes the human cost of slavery by describing Fanyah, a bright young African girl, who was captured by slavers as a child, escaped, was sold into slavery, and finally was rescued by the British. In addition, to illustrate the good that Britain is doing in Sierra Leone, Mrs. Melville remarks on the intelligence and the educational progress of African children in mission schools.

Despite its antislavery bias, however, *A Residence at Sierra Leone* is not a polemical work but a detailed reconstruction of the external and internal worlds of a white woman in nineteenth-century Africa, the deadly Paradise. The colors and textures of Sierra Leone are made palpable in descriptions that are Keatsian in their luxurious sensuousness: "mingled in one rich mass of harmonious colouring, and flinging their sweet scent to the welcome sea-breeze, orange and lime trees, spangled with snowy flowers, and bending under the weight of their gorgeous fruit vie with . . . the luxuriant mango, the bay-leaved coffee, the pale-stemmed guava, the dark densely-foliaged rose-apple" (226).

The beauties of the exotic plants, birds, and insects, which Mrs. Melville lovingly describes, can, however, neither mask nor compensate for the inherent terror of Africa, the "indefinable dread" that a foreigner experiences in this merciless climate. Isolated, often ill, threatened by hurricanes, and surrounded by "savage noises"—"the incessant beating of tom toms, the firing of muskets, the shouting and singing of the black population . . . the yelping, howling, and squealing of a horde of half-starved dogs and pigs" (122)—the European often sinks into a debilitating depression.

This depression, heightened by the ubiquity of death in Sierra Leone, effected a profound psychological change in Mrs. Melville, a change which she eloquently but unselfconsciously recorded in her narrative. When she first arrived Mrs. Melville was an eager student of her new land, ready to minimize its dangers and to laugh over the "minor inconveniences" of domestic life—the bugs, the mold, the climate, the servants (31). Gradually, she was overwhelmed by the "anxiety and suffering" caused by the very climate that produced so much natural beauty. The splendors of nature palled and even became sinister: "the great lone hills . . . looked as if they would fain repulse, by their frowning and desolate aspect, all wanderers from another land" (177). Homesick, Mrs. Melville began to long for the safe, familiar terrain of England; but when she finally returned there after nearly seven years in Africa, her sensibility had so altered that "gloomy anticipations" marred her joy at homecoming.

Like most travel books, *A Residence at Sierra Leone* sketches a world of experience bounded by two voyages; in this book, however, the distance traversed between those voyages is psychological rather than physical. Having travelled to a kind of natural paradise in which death and disease are the price of beauty, Mrs. Melville perceived and recorded the ephemerality of life and of happiness. Her journey to Africa, like that of Marlow in Conrad's *Heart of Darkness,* was an initiation into the dark underside of human life.

Harriet Ward. In the 1840s another British woman, an Army wife, reluctantly but dutifully accompanied her husband to Africa and narrated her experiences in a two-volume work entitled *Five Years in Kaffirland* (1848). Southeastern Africa, into which Harriet Ward, her husband, and her small daughter journeyed in 1842, was a land torn by racial tension and unrest. Seven years earlier, a group of Dutch settlers had fled from English rule in the Cape Colony and trekked northward to Natal, the Transvaal, and the Orange Free State. Believers in the superiority of the white race, these "Voortrekkers" frequently came into conflict with the African peoples in their path. Tensions mounted; both Dutch and English settlers skirmished with the black populace; and in 1842 Britain annexed Natal in order to preserve peace in the area and to secure Durban, a port essential to its trade with India. When the Wards moved into this region soon after the annexation, the atmosphere was charged with hostility between the Dutch and the English as well as between blacks and whites. In the five years they spent there, the Wards witnessed a number of armed skirmishes and experienced a war between the British and the "Kaffirs" (as many nineteenth-century writers called all Africans except Hottentots and Bushmen).

The book that Mrs. Ward constructed out of her experiences in this politically tense environment comprises three different narratives intertwined: an account of domestic life in an alien setting, a history of military operations in South Africa, and a political tract. On one level, Mrs. Ward vividly re-creates the sufferings and dangers endured by a military wife. Conveyed in primitive wagons, lodged in dirty, uncomfortable rooms, she often had to bear and raise children under extreme hardship in a land where food was expensive and poor, where disease was a constant threat, and where attack by hostile Africans was an ever-present danger. Mrs. Ward's own voyage to her new home was marred by a series of chaotic and nearly disastrous experiences: she was carried past "ghastly faces" and rows of "shrieking women" on a ship sinking off Cape Town in a dramatic storm, was transported up the east coast of Africa in a filthy boat, and then was plunged into the pandemonium of an army camp near Fort Peddie: "bellowing of oxen, shouts of Hottentot drivers, screams of children . . . the mingled oaths and laughter of the soldiers" (1:60).[6] Such experiences convinced her that Her Majesty's troops in Africa received worse treatment than did the poor or criminal classes in England.

Ward's documentation of the life of a colonial soldier's family is enlivened by several dramatic portrayals of the terror and frenzy of the civilian population of a fort under attack: "Children cried and laughed alternately, women screamed, Hottentots danced and sang and swore . . . muskets were going off in all quarters . . . artillery within 300 yards of us! How the windows rattle! How the roof shivers! . . . the doors fly open, and there are— not Kaffirs—only terrified women and children" (1:245). Both the immediacy of this present-tense narrative and the climactic arrangement of the action to generate suspense testify to a degree of literary skill. But Mrs. Ward was by no means a powerful, sophisticated, or lively stylist. Her descriptions often lack color; her perceptions simply reiterate conventional wisdom. To write an entertaining account of domestic life and travel in Africa is not, in fact, her aim.

Five Years in Kaffirland is chiefly a polemic designed to praise the British soldier, document the Army's honor and heroism, and draw a negative picture of the African. Not only does she criticize the government for its failure to pay fairly or supply adequately its fighting men, she also attacks those who accuse the Army of "blood-thirstiness" against Africans in the War of the Axe (1846–1848). To answer those "fallacious reasoners . . . who romanticize about savages," Mrs. Ward first documents in excruciating detail the military history of the war and, then, refutes the portraits of "Kaffirs" drawn by philanthropic groups like the Aborigines Protection Society.

From firsthand experience, Mrs. Ward claims that Africans are not "rational beings" but demonic savages who exist on a lower plane of civilization than white men. She illustrates these views in this truly gruesome passage: "A Kaffir skin more resembles the hide of some powerful animal than the skin of a human being. Some person procured the skin of a Kaffir . . . [it was] three times the thickness of a white man's" (2:127). Such spurious evidence, combined with empirical observation of Africans' "laziness and cunning," is used to prove that the whole race is

"measured and implacable" in its savagery (1:179). The implication is clear: British troops were justified in whatever actions
they might have taken against such foes. In fact, "no other country
but England would have treated a savage foe with such lenity,
forbearance, and humanity as we have done" (1:233). But toward
the end of the narrative Mrs. Ward's attitude toward Africans
softens: they become "noble animals" who need the "wholesome
restraint" of a civilized, Christian nation. This conception of the
relation between Africa and Britain, this conviction that Providence has destined Britain to colonize and civilize a backward,
heathen land, is fundamental to Victorian imperialism. Significantly, Harriet Ward urges her nation to intervene in Africa and
rule its people directly; she also encourages the immigration of
new colonists, particularly the starving Irish.

Harriet Ward, then, was a political writer who, at a time when
her nation was cautious about extending its hegemony in Africa,
argued for a full-scale commitment. Her aims in writing a narrative of her African experiences are to set the record straight
about the Army and to influence public opinion and governmental
policy. She boldly criticizes influential humanitarian groups,
dictates to the government what laws ought to be passed to
control the natives, and advocates a cold-blooded military policy:
"if we had not the heart to shoot the Kaffirs into subjection, they
might have been starved into humility" (1:139).

Yet, despite her aggressive pronouncements and strident tone,
Mrs. Ward tries to create a demure and femininely unassertive
persona. Thus, she demurs: "I have so great a dislike, as a woman,
to touch on what ought to be done anywhere, that I feel a great
reluctance to speak of public matters connected with this colony"
(1:96). Anxious not to be considered "unfeminine," she assures
readers that she "would not abdure [sic] for the world" her "wom-
anly attributes" (1:156). And, in a passage illustrating the struggle between female role and personal ambition, Ward claims that
"the head of a brigade in array for the fields is [not] an eligible
place for ladies," but that she did ride out with such a brigade
and found the experience exhilarating (1:179). Clearly, she was
troubled by the conflict between the restrictions of traditionally

ladylike behavior and the new possibilities for action and political influence available to the woman in Africa. Ironically, it was an African who first perceived this conflict. Hearing Mrs. Ward speak, he queried, "How is it that white women speak with the minds of men?" (2:260). In *Five Years in Kaffirland* the tension between an assertive, opinionated masculine persona and an apologetic, ladylike female voice reveals the problem of self-definition faced not only by Harriet Ward but, fifty years later, by Mary Kingsley as well.

The lady who spoke with a man's mind was by no means silent after writing *Five Years in Kaffirland*. The success of this book, which was praised by the *Naval and Military Gazette* as the "fullest, clearest, and most impartial account of . . . the recent war," prompted Mrs. Ward to issue an abridged version in 1851, as a handbook for would-be settlers. In addition, she began writing novels like *Helen Charteris* (1848), *Jasper Lyle* (1851), and *Lizzy Dorian, the Soldier's Wife* (1854), which incorporated her knowledge of and prejudices about the land that for five years had been her home.

The Housewives: Lady Barker, Mrs. Hutchinson, Mrs. Barkly. Mrs. Melville and Mrs. Ward were among the earliest female writers about life in Africa. By the 1870s many other wives had journeyed to the continent and written narratives, often in the form of a series of letters to a specifically female audience; these letters chronicle the domestic trials and triumphs of the housewife in Africa. Their motives for writing are aptly described by John Faragher in his discussion of women on the American Overland Trail: "the loneliness, isolation, and dread of loss that women felt frequently brought to mind friends they had left behind."[7] As their husbands maintained Britain's honor and advanced that nation's interests in Africa, these women upheld national prestige by attempting to establish civilized British homes on the shores of Lake Tanganyika or in the South African veld. Often their narratives betray more about the lives, responsibilities, and self-perceptions of Victorian wives than they do about Africa, which is sometimes merely an exotic backdrop to their domestic dramas.

Lady M. A. Barker, who had lived in New Zealand and written *Station Amusements in New Zealand* (1873), is preoccupied in *A Year's Housekeeping in South Africa* (1877) with the "bold and hideous appearance" of her house in Maritzburg, the amusing incompetence of servants, the antics of her small son, and the almost insuperable "difficulties in one's culinary path" (92).[8] Africa enters the narrative chiefly through Lady Barker's complaints about its impossible climate. Ironically, it is the exotic setting of these domestic tales that occasions their publication and commands a readership. After all, what nineteenth-century reader would pick up an account of the trials of a housewife in Manchester or Basingstoke? But what reader could resist a narrative, in the great tradition of *Robinson Crusoe,* of ingenious housekeeping adapted to the difficulties of a hostile land?

The women conceive of themselves primarily as domestic creatures, and their narratives affirm the traditional Victorian notion of a woman's proper sphere (while simultaneously depicting women who are impelled by circumstances to transcend the bounds of domesticity). Like American frontier women, most women travellers to Africa do not openly challenge the established sexual roles; but they do begin to develop "masculine" personality traits and gain some influence and power by virtue of their physical courage and endurance.[9] As a result, their narratives, which document the heroism of colonial wives and celebrate specifically female experience and perception, betray a feminism of which their authors are largely unconscious. Lady Barker's book was singled out for praise because she depicts "so much that no man would ever have seen . . . in a light so different from that in which men would have seen it."[10]

In addition, these narratives often describe the female networks that helped colonial women to survive the physical and psychological trials of African life. Mrs. Ward encounters such a network when she visits a woman who has just given birth to her fourth child while travelling across South Africa in an army wagon: the "kind voices and ready hands" of other women cheer the new mother, preventing her from "repining at the fatigue and trouble she has endured" (82). Significantly, in the books by these female travellers, male characters are conspicuously absent: the authors' husbands—the ostensible reasons why these women are in Africa in the first place—are shadowy figures whose professions, personalities, and even names are omitted or relegated to a minor position. Lady Barker, for instance, never tells us her husband's name or his professional reason for being in Africa. Instead, she explores her own psychological responses to the new post, tracing in the course of the year her gradual reconciliation to life in Africa. Even the structure of her book underlines the personal odyssey she recounts. Beginning with the journey to the new, strange land and ending with her return to her house at Maritzburg after a brief vacation, the narrative implicitly contrasts her attitudes on these two journeys. By the end she has come to accept Africa as truly her home.

The extent to which female sojourners in Africa identify this land as home is in part determined by their sympathy for and understanding of the Africans among whom they live. Lady Barker genuinely likes Africans, although she voices the common complaint about their incompetence as servants. "Kaffirs" seem to her gay, good-humored, and civil people; Zulus she finds handsome and fascinating. Her pedestrian prose style becomes rhythmical and striking as she depicts a Zulu witch, clad in lynx skins and wild beasts' teeth, creeping with a "cat-like gesture, bent double, as if she were seeking out a trail. Every movement of her undulating body kept time to the beat of the girls' hands. . . ." (173). Her fascination with the Zulu people foreshadows the romanticization they will undergo in the 1880s by the novelist Rider Haggard and the traveller Lady Florence Dixie. Although Lady Barker never becomes a passionate advocate of the Zulu like Florence Dixie, she does urge her government to restrict white immigration to South Africa, allowing into the colony only those who have skills to teach Africans. Convinced that she knows the conditions in Africa more intimately than administrators at home, she advocates a policy that she feels will reduce racial tensions and benefit Africans.

The housekeeping problems of a British wife in Africa are magnified when her "house" is an army tent; but Louisa Hutchinson's jolly narrative of domestic life in a military camp, *In Tents in the Transvaal* (1879), minimizes personal discomforts and inconveniences. Cast as a series of letters home, her book sparkles with that immediacy and unaffected freshness of style prized by Victorian readers of travel books. A lover of adventure, Mrs. Hutchinson left her baby in England to travel with her husband to Utrecht in the Transvaal near Zululand. Although she did not realize it at the time, Mrs. Hutchinson was witnessing the prelude to a dramatic military encounter between British forces and the Zulu nation. In April 1877 the Administrator of the British colony of Natal, Theophilus Shepstone, had annexed the Afrikaner-controlled Transvaal thereby enmeshing Britain in the long-standing feud between the Afrikaner and the Zulu over land. To placate the restive Boers by convincing them that their new government "had a sound view of race relations and the strength to enforce its decisions,"[11] the British invaded Zululand in 1879. Mrs. Hutchinson's narrative, which was published during the year of the war, had a unique popular appeal because it "render[ed] more distinct and clear that . . . unfamiliar country which English men and women are trying to bring before their imaginations at this moment" (221).[12]

Mrs. Hutchinson, however, is no supporter of the war whose prelude she witnessed; in fact, she bluntly criticizes British imperial policy which is forcing the Zulus into an unwanted war. In ironic tones she also questions her nation's methods of "civilizing" Africans: "It must be hoped . . . that the Kaffirs will . . . cheerfully suffer themselves to be missionized, shot, and bayoneted into tail-coats, mahogany, and trial by jury. They must see—that is—be made to see that it is better to be improved, even if needs be off the face of the earth, than to remain in their present condition of barbarous, if blissful, ignorance" (125). Furthermore, she challenges the propagandists' portrait of the Zulu King Cetshwayo (also spelled "Cetewayo") as a "blood-thirsty despot." Noting that their camp is poorly guarded and close to the border with Zululand, Mrs. Hutchinson concludes that, if Cetshwayo "were half as treacherous and bloodthirsty as his would-be enemies pretend," he would already have annihilated them (158). Like Florence Dixie, who travelled through Zululand four years later and returned convinced of British injustice, Mrs. Hutchinson perceives and criticizes the hypocritical politics of her nation. The people whom politicians depict as aggressive, cruel savages, she finds to be dignified, attractive, and good-humored. In fact, like other British women travellers she prefers Africans to the Boers, the Dutch farmers of South Africa.

Despite her candid criticisms of British policy, Louisa Hutchinson's book is not a political diatribe but a domestic comedy with Africa as its setting and a charming, witty, inventive young Army wife as its protagonist. Although, like most travellers, Mrs. Hutchinson feels obliged to describe scenery, to comment on the discomforts of travel, and to discourse on the customs of "the natives," she is chiefly interested in recording the daily life of the Army: the bustling chaos of an early morning decampment; the wearisome routine of a hot day's march; the monotony of life in an isolated, barren military outpost where there is nothing to read, to sew, or to cook, and where the only creative outlet is "the Mephistophelian art of killing time" (173). Like other housewives in Africa, Mrs. Hutchinson chronicles her domestic tribulations to an audience presumed to be sympathetic to her struggle to find decent food or invent tasty recipes for cooking unpalatable ingredients.

Unlike a number of other women African travellers, though, Mrs. Hutchinson always maintains a humorous, mocking tone about her trials. Experiences that others might treat as disasters, she regards as amusing interludes. Thus, trying to cook dinner in a heavy rain storm is described as "enjoying a shower bath in our clothes . . . [while] the eggs and bacon that are frying for one of our delightful (?) gypsy suppers are being rapidly converted into soup" (43). Here Louisa Hutchinson laughs not only at her predicament but at her own romantic expectations about camp life. Almost twenty years later, the African traveller Mary Kingsley will use humor, as does Mrs. Hutchinson, to minimize danger and discomfort, depicting a journey to Africa as a "lark."

Though Mrs. Hutchinson takes seriously her domestic responsibilities, the persona of her book is not chiefly a housewife but
an amusing, self-mocking adventurer. In a tent in the Transvaal
because she has gamely insisted on joining her husband at camp
rather than staying behind in a hotel, Louisa Hutchinson clearly
relishes the sometimes exciting, sometimes ludicrous predica-
ments that ensue. Jokingly, she admits that her husband, who
seldom appears in the narrative, berates her for "the lamentable
wilfulness" (43) that she displays in coming along with him; but
she is decidedly unrepentant. In sprightly prose she describes an
attempt to ride alone to camp, even though she has never before
been in the saddle: "Dashing along [the principal street of Dur-
ban] in a fine imitation of the great Gilpin, avoiding collison
with carriages and great ox waggons," Mrs. Hutchinson discovers
that she cannot stop her steed: "I twisted the reins around my
arm, round the pommel . . . round my leg, and pulled with
all my might. . ." (38). Slapstick comedy also characterizes her
description of an attempt to shoot a deer; the animal, she notes,
"did not seem half so much scared as an orderly, who . . .
evidently suspected me of suicidal intentions" (193).

Not only her own but other people's absurdities draw her
mocking scrutiny: she pokes fun at the valorous pretensions of
the soldiers, at the manners of colonials, and at the camp's cook,
a Dickensian character who talks endlessly of the legendary pud-
ding he made in 1872. Despite her claim that her narrative is
designed merely for "the amusement of an idle half-hour" (221),
Mrs. Hutchinson sometimes uses humor for political purposes.
Thus, with a dramatic flair she limns a local Dutch farmer,
Smuts, as he discusses with her husband the British annexation
of the Transvaal: " 'You would know what I tink?' [Smuts says]
. . . shaking his great heavy head and frowning, till his red
little pig eyes disappear into twinkling points of light. 'Ah, but
I have not de language . . . I support the Boers in a rising,
rebellion, how do you call it? You see, I speak so vera, vera leetle
English' " (169). Hers is a prophetic portrait, for Smuts's canny
evasiveness and his opposition to British rule foreshadow future
political trouble. Two years after this conversation the Boers did

rebel against the British. Mrs. Hutchinson's comic odyssey, *In Tents in the Transvaal*, is then an inadvertently political book which not only challenges some popular ideas about Britain's presumed enemy, the Zulu, but also portrays her potential enemy, the Boer.

In the late 1870s yet another British wife followed her husband to Southern Africa, but Fanny Barkly found little to joke about in her narrative of suffering, privation, and warfare, *Among Boers and Basutos* (1893). Isolated at a remote outpost in Basutoland (Lesotho) without a doctor, a clergyman, or another white woman, Mrs. Barkly experienced the lonely drudgery of a colonial wife who was in charge of child care, cooking, housework, farming, milling, and a host of other chores. As the family grew and a rift developed between the British and the Basuto, her burdens only increased.

Concerned about the British treatment of the Zulu and angry at an ordinance requiring all Africans to surrender their weapons, a group of Basutos under Lerothodi rebelled in 1878 and the "Gun War" began. The historical drama in which she unwittingly participates enlivens Fanny Barkly's otherwise flat narrative. Her home at Mafeteng is attacked; seriously ill after the birth of her fourth child, she must flee by night to the Orange Free State, where for months she struggles to find food and fuel for herself and her children. Exhausted by stress and by late-night copying of military despatches smuggled out of her besieged home, she collapses, only to be required, upon recovery, to care for a son seriously injured in an accident and a husband ill from a severe chill. Her tale of woe ends when her husband is ordered home; the final entry in the book is his letter of resignation, offered to the reader without comment.

But, despite its vivid re-creation of the suffering of a civilian population at the war front and its value as a historical record, *Among Boers and Basutos* is a seriously flawed book. The style is unimaginative, the diction conventional and lifeless, the narrative diffusive. Because she has chosen to include not only her own journal entries, but excerpts of her husband's letters to his father about politics, military despatches, and newspaper reports of battles, Mrs. Barkly's narrative is disjointed, the chronological sequence of events confusing. The world of personal experience never integrates with that of historical events. Nevertheless, *Among Boers and Basutos* was a popular work, passing through three editions between 1893 and 1896. Mrs. Barkly went on to write another narrative of her subsequent life as the wife of a diplomat in the Seychelles and Helgoland, *From the Tropics to the North Sea* (1897).

Missionaries

Background. A sense of adventure or of marital duty brought some women to Africa; the hope of eradicating heathenism, savagery, and ignorance lured others. These missionaries and wives of missionaries often sent home narratives of their labors, which served not only to publicize missionary work in Africa but also to elicit financial contributions for missionary societies. Thus the Wesleyan Methodist missionaries were instructed to "keep a journal, and to send home frequently such copious extracts as may give full and particular account of . . . labours, success, and prospects."[13]

From the 1830s on, missionary narratives proliferated. Perhaps the most famous of these, David Livingstone's *Missionary Travels* (1857), is both an account of his pioneering journey across Africa (1853–1856) and a clarion call to "all young missionaries to go at once to the real heathen."[14] Through his writings, lectures, and personal example, Livingstone sparked the public's interest in Africa and advanced a set of ideas about trade that influenced the course of future missionary activities. He believed that civilization and trade went hand in hand, that contact with white people would improve the moral status of Africans, and that slavery could be combated if African trading opportunities were expanded and the economic base of African society broadened. Inspired by his vision, Oxford, Cambridge, Edinburgh, and Durham Universities formed a missionary group which eventually established a station in the Shiré Highlands of Malawi; the Scottish church sent missionaries to the area around Lake Nyasa and launched a trading steamer on the lake in 1876; and Livingstone's own parent organization, the London Missionary Society, sent an exploratory party to Lake Tanganyika in the same year to determine if a missionary settlement could survive at Ujiji.

From the ventures of the Scottish Mission and the London Missionary Society came three narratives by women: Mrs. M. A. Pringle's *Towards the Mountains of the Moon* (1884), Annie M. Hore's *To Lake Tanganyika in a Bath Chair* (1886), and Jane Moir's *A Lady's Letters from Central Africa* (1891). To emphasize the need for proselytizing, the typical nineteenth-century missionary narrative often drew shocking or sensational portraits of the unconverted African—portraits which betrayed the author's own "cultural chauvinism." But the books by these three women, while they generally support the efforts of missionaries, do not denigrate or stereotype black people; instead, they present rather sympathetic human portraits of individual Africans.

M. A. Pringle.   The most entertaining, least typical of these narratives is *Towards the Mountains of the Moon,* a work based on Mrs. Pringle's letters to her family in England. The book's picturesque title, an allusion to Ptolemy's belief that the Nile's source lay "in the mountains of the moon" just north of the equator, indicates that the narrative will be neither conventional nor pedestrian. Perhaps the book's uniqueness arises from the fact that neither Mrs. Pringle nor her husband was a missionary.

In 1880 Alexander Pringle, a member of the Established Church of Scotland, was sent to East Africa to investigate conditions at the Blantyre Mission and determine the cause of the reported friction between missionaries and local clans. His wife was determined to accompany him as far as she could, even though she was cautioned that "a lady can never manage the journey up the African rivers" (5).[15] But bewildered officials were no match for the persistent Mrs. Pringle, as she humorously observes: "nobody knew what to do with me; they would pass me on to their neighbours who in their turn would do the same" (53). This amused detachment toward adventure characterizes Mrs. Pringle's narrative; like Louisa Hutchinson, she creates the persona of an intrepid and ironic traveller who finds Africa entertaining. Her first harrowing night on the river journey to

Blantyre, for example, affords amusement: "Before we could become used to the dim light of the lantern, we were startled by a tremendous yell and instantaneously the boat received a great push . . . into the middle of the river, nearly capsizing us. We were now quite in the hands of the savages . . . [and] we could do nothing but laugh at our own novel predicament" (94). Mrs. Pringle, like Louisa Hutchinson or Mary Kingsley, uses laughter to control fear and distance danger. For instance, when she is suddenly and unexpectedly picked up and carried off by an African porter, she does not scream: she laughs—so astonishing the black man that he nearly pitches her into the surrounding bush (320).

Mrs. Pringle's humor also manifests itself as an ironic self-distance. Conscious of the two audiences for whom she plays—her readers and the people among whom she travels—she sometimes dramatizes to one audience her performance before another. She opens her letter of 5 September 1883 with the spectacle of herself sitting "à la Turk" (cross-legged) under a thatched roof while the entire female population of the village watches her attempt to write this letter. Moreover, acutely aware of her effect on Africans, many of whom have never seen a white woman before, Mrs. Pringle alternates between amusement at their bewilderment and dismay at their fear. "Imagine," she exclaims, "the strangeness of realizing oneself to be a hobgoblin" (165).

Able to see herself as she appears to others, Mrs. Pringle can look sympathetically at Africans and their culture, eschewing popular stereotypes. She finds black people "reticent and sensitive" (193), fun-loving, and "industrious" (214)—a far cry from the lazy savages of the myths. As a woman she is distressed by the grief of mothers whose children have been abducted into slavery: "beating the floor and singing the wail . . . for hours and hours, drawing the most vivid pictures of their poor children" (246). Her sympathy also includes a respect for African cultural institutions. Consequently, she is critical of those missionaries who try to extirpate local culture or who wantonly ignore African mores. Such chauvinistic attitudes have been responsible, she insists, for the failure of the Blantyre mission.

Although *Towards the Mountains of the Moon* purports to be nothing more than an unpretentious narrative of "a few weeks' life among the natives" (x), it is in actuality a book with educational and political dimensions. Like many missionary narratives, it documents the history of a mission settlement; but, unlike them, it analyzes the problems that can beset such a venture when missionaries lack knowledge of and sympathy for local culture. To combat ignorance about Africa, Mrs. Pringle presents information on the history and culture of certain African peoples, based both on observation and on scholarly reading; moreover, she openly disputes some of Livingstone's influential notions about the African's natural orientation toward trading and about the symbiosis of trade and civilization. Like Mary Kingsley's *Travels in West Africa,* Mrs. Pringle's book successfully blends humorous narrative of a series of "scrapes" with some serious, semi-scholarly information about the land and peoples of Africa.

Annie B. Hore.   Two years after Mrs. Pringle's landmark journey, Annie Hore, her husband, infant son, and eight missionaries from the London Missionary Society set out from England for the shores of Lake Tanganyika. Captain Hore had already spent three years surveying the lake and had concluded that Europeans could safely live in the interior of Africa (2).[16] The story of the Hores' attempts to reach the region around Lake Tanganyika and to verify Captain Hore's conclusions about its suitability as a dwelling place is contained in Mrs. Hore's *To Lake Tanganyika in a Bath Chair* (1886), a book intended, as its author admits, "to awaken interest in our mission in new quarters."[17] Even her choice of title, an intriguing allusion to the unique palanquin Captain Hore designed for his wife and son, indicates that Mrs. Hore wants to attract a reading public not usually inclined toward mission publications.

The first half of the book narrates the harrowing experiences that beset the expedition from the beginning: the steamboat, which the party was to carry in parts to the lake and then assemble, was late in arriving from England; Mrs. Hore was stricken by sunstroke and inflammation of the liver; the rainy season, when travel is virtually impossible, approached before the group could leave Zanzibar. Rather than risk the failure of his "experiment" designed to prove that women and children could travel in Africa, Captain Hore sent his family home and proceeded with the missionaries to Ujiji on Lake Tanganyika. The Hores agreed to meet in a year to attempt the journey again, this time by a water route from Quelimane to Lake Nyasa and then on to Tanganyika. This attempt was also frustrated by an African uprising. Finally, in September 1884, almost two years after their first arrival, the Hores began the long, painful overland journey through drought-stricken East Africa.

In the preface of her book Mrs. Hore promises her readers a narrative of "my views of scenes and adventures (for the first time witnessed and experienced by one of my own sex) which . . . have been thought of thrilling interest and importance" (1). Yet her narrative is neither thrilling nor particularly personal. Situations that might evoke strong pity or horror are rendered in a dry, impersonal, understated prose. A traumatic journey through war-torn country to join a husband whose whereabouts were unknown is characterized as "altogether the most tedious and painful of my African experiences" (40). Similarly, in a matter-of-fact tone, she records that on the journey to Tanganyika, her party found some "curious dark objects" in the road—"the hardened and preserved" bodies of porters from slave caravans who had died of starvation. Simply noting that these were "terrible" sights, Mrs. Hore eschews lurid description, instead launching into an impassioned lecture on the evils of slavery. The rapid shift here from pallid narration to fierce polemic reveals the true intent of Mrs. Hore's book—the promotion of missionary labors and the demonstration that women can travel and live in Africa. To this end, she carefully underplays her physical privations and anxieties during a journey that was nearly fatal to her son. But, ironically, since the appeal of her book to the lay reading public lies in its account of dangerous adventures of a woman in remote Africa, Mrs. Hore cannot totally omit painful or sensational experiences.

Although she understates her own sufferings, Mrs. Hore sympathetically recounts the hardships endured by the large party of porters, who struggle in the heat with little water and even less food. Despite her compassion for them, however, Mrs. Hore subscribes to the popular estimation of Africans as "passionate children" who thoughtlessly "maul" each other and need an "adult power" (like Christian Britain) to civilize them and insure their safety (168). Since she believes in the cultural inferiority of Africans—which she partly attributes to the slave trade—Mrs. Hore shows little interest in the culture of the peoples among whom she lives. She simply observes that Africans "have their own distinct ideas of order, independence, and morals" (162). After all, she had come to Africa in order to alter that indigenous morality.

Once the Hore family arrived in Tanganyika and began to establish a home and a school on Kavala Island, Mrs. Hore's narrative changes pace, sounding increasingly like the books by housewives. The quotidian details of finding a healthy spot, building a house, planting a garden, and learning to live with the Waguha tribe on the island dominate her account. The climate is unhealthy, building materials are difficult to find, and the missionary endures extreme psychological pressure. In a rare, unguarded moment she betrays the strain of life in Africa: "It is not without effort . . . that civilization is retained to ourselves. . . . It is not impossible for isolated representatives of civilization to be swamped in savagedom" (189). However, it is not Annie Hore but Joseph Conrad who dramatizes and explores, in stories like "An Outpost of Progress" and *The Heart of Darkness,* the psychological horror of being "swamped in savagedom." Mrs. Hore concludes her book on a determinedly optimistic note after the family has lived in Africa for a year: "we have fairly well proved the healthiness of the situation. . . . I have now fully taken charge of household duties. . . . Jack has almost fully recovered. . . . All round the Lake healthy sites are to be found, where it is hoped to establish situations" (208). This statement, with its repeated qualifications—"almost" and "fairly"—is followed by a plea to those at home interested in "emancipating" Africans from "the chains of depravity, ignorance, and slavery" to join the missionary ranks in Africa. But Mrs. Hore has not told the full truth about her situation in this propagandistic conclusion. She has omitted the physical and mental hardships under which the missionaries labored in that first year, the deaths which had diminished their numbers, and her husband's growing weariness and frustration. In March 1885 Captain Hore, plagued by "the usual sequel of fevers . . . rheumatism . . . ulcers, etc." and by "nervous disappointment," wrote to the Secretary of the London Missionary Society that he planned to retire soon from Africa. [18] In October 1885 one of the missionaries at Ujiji, distressed that his companions were "falling one after the other," wrote that "Europeans are not qualified physically for the climate of this part of Africa." [19] And in June 1886 the mission's committee voted to abandon the station. The Tanganyika mission, however, survived this crisis and the Hores remained there until 1888, when Captain Hore was forced by ill health to leave Africa. His final letter to the London Missionary Society announces his resignation and his intention of moving with his family to Tasmania, where he will use his engineering skill in industry. Of his wife, who had suffered for and had written in support of the missionary cause, no more was heard. All that remains is her undramatic narrative of some exotic and trying experiences in a book that has become "a classic in its own way." [20]

Jane Moir.   In 1890 another women associated with a missionary venture journeyed through central Africa and even visited Kavala Island where the Hores had resided. Jane Moir, wife of Frederick Moir, the director of the African Lakes Company, travelled from Mandala in the Shiré highlands to Lake Tanganyika and then back home along the shores of Lake Nyasa. Her chatty, informal letters written on this journey were published in 1891 under the title *A Lady's Letters from Central Africa*. Superficially Mrs. Moir resembled Mrs. Hore: both were wives of men responsible for the practical, rather than the spiritual, side of a mission venture. Edward Hore was an engineer whose time was spent assembling, repairing, and sailing a steamer; Frederick Moir, a merchant, who in 1876 launched a steamer on Lake Nyasa in an attempt to use the ivory trade as a weapon against the Arab traffic in slaves. But in temperament and in literary style these women are strikingly different. Despite some discomforts and an attack by Africans seeking ivory, Mrs. Moir regards her 240-mile odyssey through central Africa as "the very pleasantest journey that two mortals can have" (31);[21] she finds camp life "charming," the company jovial, and the scenery breathtaking. With an eye for detail and a sense of humor lacking in Annie Hore, Jane Moir re-creates entertaining social scenes: the bustle of the Ujiji market, the daily routine of an Arab household, the impertinence of harem women who invade her chambers and beg for sweets. The book even contains some charming, primitive sketches which she drew for her daughter in England.

Mrs. Moir has no ulterior motive in writing her narrative; she neither propagandizes for the missions nor berates Africans for their primitivism and savagery. In fact, she is frank in her admiration for a kind of paradise that she finds on the North Coast of Lake Nyasa, where the naked black men are "magnificent, the larger portion of them being over six feet high and splendidly made" (79). Unabashedly she admits that, were it not for the exigencies of trade, she would like all Africans to go naked with "clean, well-oiled bodies" (84). This easy frankness about a subject that a Victorian lady would not ordinarily discuss testifies both to the unusual experiential license afforded the woman in Africa and to the freedom of expression possible in letters addressed to a familial audience.

While Mrs. Moir offers no new geographical, scientific, or ethnological information and advances no political arguments, she does provide a fresh, unaffected narrative of how Africa can alter a woman's self-perception. She relates that, in one village, the natives cannot believe that she is a woman because "she has no stomach; how can she be so thin if she is a woman?" (27). After trying to explain that differences in clothing produce this confusion, Mrs. Moir confesses that "if it weren't for fear of sunstrokes and a few other difficulties, I would like very much to dress in a big bath towel, and then probably I would be much admired" (27). Amused by cultural differences, Mrs. Moir can humorously contemplate something that would have been unthinkable to Harriet Ward fifty years earlier. And she can experience the journey through a wild, uncivilized land as a delightful vacation.

Vacationers

Mrs. Moir, writing late in the century, describes the pleasures of a leisurely tour, not the rigors of a daring journey or the trials of a pioneering life; by the 1880s and 1890s, hardy vacationers as well as serious, professional travellers began to make their way to Africa. Drawn by the climate or by the novelty of visiting so distant a place, these travellers exemplify the truth of Mrs. Oliphant's observation that an English traveller "now must go to the extremities of the earth before he will find any region which it is creditable and novel to have visited."[22]

One such vacationer is Alice Balfour, who in 1884 set off with her brother, the Right Honorable A. J. Balfour, and two friends, to traverse Matabeleland and Mashunaland by wagon. In a light-hearted, superficial, epistolary narrative, *Twelve Hundred Miles in a Waggon* (1895) Miss Balfour recounts a journey which other people deemed "crazy" but which she enjoyed: "except for the dust and dirt and the hurry, there are very few drawbacks to the life" (102).[23] As a travel writer, Miss Balfour is more interested in the daily life of the itinerant vacationer than in the worlds that travel unfolds. At the beginning of her narrative, she warns readers that she will eschew the political and social problems of the countries through which she passes, the towns that have previously been described by travellers, and the personal significance of the journey. What remains after such radical omissions are hackneyed observations on the scenery, stereotypical portraits of Africans and Boers, and humorless descriptions of life in a South African wagon.

In contrast, Lucie Duff Gordon, the beautiful socialite, translator, and literary hostess, who some claim was the prototype of Ida in Tennyson's *The Princess,* wrote a series of letters about her travels in South Africa that epitomize many of the best features of travel writing by women. Chatty, informal, and occasionally humorous, her *Letters from the Cape* (1864) dramatize the liberating effect of travel on a woman and provide vividly detailed portraits of the people and scenes that she encounters.

Like Isabella Bird or Hester Stanhope, Lucie Duff Gordon travelled for her health, seeking a climate in which her tuberculosis could be cured. And like these famed women travellers, she discovered that travel was physically and psychologically exhilarating: "No one can conceive what it is, after two years of prison and utter languor, to stand on the top of a mountain pass, and enjoy physical existence for a few hours" (315).[24] The vital, witty narrative persona that Mrs. Duff Gordon creates in these letters to her family, written in 1861–1862, celebrates the "enchanted wonder" that she feels in the face of "new birds and beasts and people" (305). Her attempt to regain good health in the South African sun affords Lucie Duff Gordon the opportunity for another restoration, a "second youth" (305).

With the enthusiasm of a child, Mrs. Duff Gordon relishes even the trying or painful aspects of travel; moreover, she vividly captures the human comedy of life in the small colonial towns she visits. Of a New Year's celebration at a small hotel in Calendon, she writes:

Then came a Dutchman and asked for six penn'orth of "brood en kaas" and haggled for beer; and Englishmen, who bought chickens and champagne without asking the price. One rich old Boer got three lunches and then "trekked" . . . without paying at all. Then came a Hottentot, stupidly drunk, with a fiddle and was beaten by a little red-haired Scotchman and his fiddle smashed. (253)

Mrs. Duff Gordon's interest in people extends to the Malays and Africans whom she treats with a respect that wins their friendship. To her the Malays seem handsome, agreeable, and pleasant companions; moreover, she is frequently struck by the physical beauty of Africans. One pregnant African woman takes on mythical proportions in her description: "Her jet black face was like a Sphynx [*sic*], . . . her shape and walk were goddess-like" (214). Her sympathy for the black and colored peoples of Africa leads Mrs. Duff Gordon to a remorseful consciousness of what her race has done to Africa's rightful possessors. Standing before a 107-year-old man, who claimed to be the last living Hottentot, she begins to feel like "a tyrant and oppressor" (270). Repeatedly in her letters she criticizes the behavior and attitudes of white people toward blacks. She blames Dutch slavery for debasing many black men, turning them into sulky drunkards. She condemns not only Afrikaner injustice to Africans but also British "contemptuousness" of black and colored people. She censures the cultural chauvinism of British thought: "have we grown so *very* civilized . . . that outlandish people seem like mere puppets . . . [not] real human beings?" (29 January 1864). [25] Sympathetic to the outlandish but intriguing people she met in South Africa—and later in Egypt—Mrs. Duff Gordon, like a number of other women travellers, found through travel a mission that engaged her sympathies, her intellect, and her literary skills. In *Letters from the Cape* (1862–1863) and the later *Letters from Egypt* (1863–1869), she argues for the humanity of exploited peoples and condemns the callous inhumanity of their colonial oppressors.

Whether they went to Africa for pleasure or because of a duty to God or man, women travellers shared some common experiences and produced books which, though widely variant in literary sophistication, objectivity, precision, and humor, seem to possess cognate personae—hardy, inquisitive creatures who endure privations with few complaints. Their travel books contain little of the carefully observed anthropological detail of Mary Kingsley's writings but do often reveal a particular sympathy for Africans and sometimes even advocate governmental action to insure the well-being of African peoples. In addition, this long-neglected body of writing by women frequently records rites of passage that female travellers underwent in Africa. For these women, as for Florence Dixie and Mary Kingsley, Africa often yielded a new knowledge—of themselves, of the world, of life itself.

Chapter Three
Florence Douglas Dixie
The Early Years

I wonder what the early thoughts of man would be if the position of the sexes were reversed, when he first realized the fact that secret contempt of sex was the reason for the disabilities imposed on him by woman. I know, speaking as a woman, that when I first opened my eyes as a girl on those disabilities, and realized that my sex was the barrier that hid from my yearning gaze the bright fields of activity, usefulness, and reform, the bitterness and pain that entered into my soul can never be obliterated in my lifetime. Child as I was, I resolved to defy those unnatural laws. . . . [1]

From the beginning, defiance was indeed the keynote of the life of Florence Douglas Dixie, an unconventional woman who grew from a lithe, blond tomboy into a famous world traveller, big-game hunter, war correspondent, author, lecturer, feminist, and political activist. Born in 1857, Florence was one of a pair of twins, the youngest of the six children of Archibald William Douglas, the seventh Marquis of Queensbury, and Caroline Margaret Clayton, daughter of General Sir William Robert Clayton. The Douglas clan traced its ancestry to a number of proud, pugnacious Scotsmen, among whom were Sir William Douglas, the compatriot of Wallace in his 1297 uprising against the English, and James Douglas, friend of Robert the Bruce, who died fighting the Saracens in Spain while on the way to the Holy Land carrying his dead king's heart. Adventure, political involvement, violent death, and temperamental volatility seemed to be a Douglas legacy. When Florence was three, her father shot himself while cleaning a gun; several years later, her eighteen-year-old brother was killed in the first English attempt to scale the Matterhorn; her beloved twin James committed suicide in a fit of depression in 1891. Finally, her nephew Alfred Douglas was Oscar Wilde's lover and her brother John Sholto, the eighth Marquis of Queensbury, was Wilde's opponent in the infamous law suit.

A fearless, adventurous child, Florence Douglas joined her brothers in their boisterous physical exercise—racing, climbing trees, wrestling, riding bareback. She later asserted that the physical freedom she had experienced made her "strong, hardy, active, and able to endure any amount of physical or mental fatigue."[2] Indeed, it was excellent training for the woman who was to travel on horseback for days, sleep outdoors, and hunt for food in Patagonia and South Africa. In addition, it molded a fiercely independent personality contemptuous of Victorian ideas about women's capacity or natural role. Florence Douglas's life seems to illustrate Mary Wollstonecraft's observation that women who display "vigour of intellect" and rationality in adulthood have been "allowed to run wild" as children.[3]

But Florence Dixie's childhood was not an unmitigated idyll of freedom and closeness to nature. Not only did she lose a father, she was nearly separated from her mother as well. In the thinly disguised autobiographical novel *The Story of Ijain, or the Evolution of a Mind* (1903), she describes how her mother converted to Catholicism, to the chagrin of the children's guardians who threatened to take away Lady Douglas's children. In an age when women had no legal right to their own progeny, Lady Douglas had no option but to flee, taking the seven-year-old twins with her to France. This early trauma undoubtedly contributed to Florence Douglas's later indignation at the injustice done to women in Britain.

After two years in France, the Douglas family returned to England where Florence was enrolled in a convent school. A rebellious spirit, she hated the school regimen, particularly the dogmatic religious instruction; moreover, she sorely missed her twin brother. The twins were reunited within a year to join their mother on an extended tour of the Continent; for the next five years, the family lived a largely nomadic existence which whetted the children's appetite for further travel.

The young Florence Douglas seems to have been a highly intelligent girl whose physical vigor was matched by an inquisitive mind. Early in life she questioned the doctrines of religion, speculating on the existence of a "lady God" and dismissing the Christian heaven as a dull place in which she could not imagine her dead father and brother. When the famous novelist George Bulwer Lytton met her in Geneva in 1872, he was struck by the "dreaming face and earnest eyes" of this pensive, other-worldly child to whom he wrote the poem "To Little Florrie Douglas."[4]

The young girl's own volume of poems, *Songs of a Child* (1901–1902), written between the ages of ten and seventeen under the pseudonym "Darling," attests to her pensive and wide-ranging mind. Though imitative in form, conventional in diction, and sometimes too sentimental for modern tastes, a number of these poems reveal a young mind willing to scrutinize its world, challenge conventional verities, and search for answers to social and metaphysical questions. This volume contains Wordsworthian reflections on nature, energetic ballads about the heroic Douglas clan, and narratives of childish adventures; but there are also works that speculate on man's relationship with nature, on the existence of God, on the horrors of war, and on a theme that recurs in Florence's writing for the next thirty years: man's oppression of his fellow creatures—both human and animal. In works like "The Union of Mercy," which urges children to abandon bird-killing and egg-stealing and adults to eschew furs, and "A Prayer for the Dogs," which pleads for humane treatment of animals, she betrays the deep sympathy for nonhuman life that eventually leads her to vegetarianism and agitation for reforms of the practice of hunting for sport. Her sympathies also extend to the other victims of man's inhumanity—the poor. In one of her most interesting early poems, "Poverty's Bitter Cry," she convincingly creates the voice of a despairing, hard-working member of the lower classes who challenges the church hierarchy: "Ye tells us in yor church / That all are equal" but clearly "we're poor muck" and God "likes the rich uns best."[5] Such satire on established religion and social injustice indicates a nascent political radicalism that will eventually blossom in her public advocacy of the cause of Zulu king Cetshwayo, of the rights of women, and of the Irish peasant.

Other poems show that, although she was raised as a Catholic, Florence Douglas evolved at an early age a personal, pantheistic religion, combining a Wordsworthian natural piety with a Shelleyan atheism. Inevitably, such political and religious views isolated her from her peers and contributed to a perception of herself as a lonely, misunderstood child. Later in life she told a friend that her pious family had tried to stamp out her unconventional views by confiscating her books, monitoring her correspondence, and banishing her to Europe. "I was a very naughty child, but I think I was more misunderstood than naughty. I was a very sensitive child too."[6] In a poem, "Be Kind to the Erring Child," she pleads for gentle and imaginative treatment of talented but defiant children. In the poem to George Bulwer Lytton which prefaces *Songs of a Child,* Florence Douglas dramatizes her isolation, praising the "endearing sympathy" of the novelist that saved her from "Despair's dark path."

Clearly, the pose of the romantic exile appealed to the passionate adolescent girl. At age thirteen she wrote *Waifs and Strays; or The Pilgrimage of a Bohemian Abroad* (published 1884), a poem clearly modelled on Byron's popular *Childe Harold's Pilgrimage.* At fifteen she again adopted a Byronic persona, making Cain the hero of a blank verse play in three acts, *Abel Avenged: A Dramatic Tragedy* (1877). A defiant, questioning spirit, Cain longs to liberate man from God-ordained ignorance and inveighs against the "cruel tyrant," God, who has fated this basically "loving and most gentle" man to sin.[7] Although the religious ideas in this work were so unconventional that the young author's teachers branded the heretical, *Abel Avenged* presents a traditional picture of the relationship between the sexes. Eva, Cain's wife, is the "guiding star and peaceful haven" for the questing male spirit; woman's power is exercised through man: "thy love shall drive men mad or make them great." Women are capable of "diffusing" a "mighty wisdom" to all of creation, but the author never specifies the nature of that particular legacy. Instead, Eva kills herself at the play's end, partly to prove her "undying love", partly to atone for the offenses that women of the future will commit in their rebellion against the oppression and shame imposed on them by society.

As *Abel Avenged* makes clear, the adolescent Florence Douglas perceived herself as a rebel in the Romantic tradition. Her mother admitted to a friend: "As a child, no one could manage her but me—at fifteen years old she sat on a window, three parts out of it over a terrible height, and threatened to throw herself down unless she could do as she pleased. . . . She has no idea of not having her own way."[8] Recalcitrant and independent, she naturally dreaded the inevitable transition from the freedom of childhood to the "manacles . . . and prisons of unnatural fashion" ("To Fashion," *Songs of a Child*) that would be imposed upon her as an adult. A woman of her class was, of course, expected to make an appearance at Court, to launch herself upon the marriage market, and to sail, after a series of parties and balls, into the safe horbor of marriage. However, the "larky"[9] young Douglas balked at such a career: she refused to wear the finery and the piled tresses required for a Court presentation and consequently earned a rebuke from the Lord Chamberlain for appearing before Queen Victoria with short hair and without the requisite finery. Undaunted, she simply avoided Court, devoting her time to active sport better suited to her temperament. She rode, shot, and even swam with her male friends, among whom was the Prince of Wales. But, although she scorned the artificialities of the marriage market, she did not scorn love and marriage.

At the age of eleven she had met in Europe a tall, handsome, reflective young midshipman six years her senior, who promised to marry her and travel with her around the world. And Alexander Beaumont Churchill Dixie, the descendant of Sir Wolston Dixie, Lord Mayor of London during Elizabeth's reign and the scion of a distinguished Leicestershire family, was as good as his word. In 1875 the eighteen-year-old Florence married the 24-year-old "Beau," who shared her love of sport and travel. Evidently, he did not share her political enthusiasm: his obituary in the *Times* (22 August 1924) notes only that he was an enthusiastic gardener and sportsman. His diaries show him to have been a phlegmatic, somewhat unimaginative man whose major passions were hunting and horse-racing. The young couple had two sons in the first three years of marriage: George Douglas (born 1876) and Albert Edward Wolston Beaumont (born 1878), the godson of the Prince of Wales. Then the children stopped—Florence Dixie later became an advocate of family planning who asserted that "the production of a large family must ruin a woman's health. . . . I declare therefore that act to be an immoral one, for it makes the woman untrue to herself" and produces sickly, diseased children. [10]

Marriage and motherhood clearly did not tame fiery Florence Douglas into a sedate Lady Dixie; rather these experiences seem to have deepened her anger at the position of women in British society. In *Abel Avenged* Dixie had celebrated woman's power "for good and evil over all the world," but she envisioned this power as active chiefly through women's influence on men. In the slightly later poem published in *Songs of a Child*, "Esterelle, the Lure Witch of the Alpine Glen," Dixie told of a beautiful young woman who murdered her stepfather and then took refuge in the Alps, where she lured other men to their deaths. Esterelle was driven to violence by her stepfather's exploitation of her mother, but the poem suggests that all women are similarly degraded by a society in which they are sold like "chattel" in marriage.

In the blark verse tragedy written soon after her own marriage, *Isola; or the Disinherited: a revolt for woman and all the disinherited* (published 1902), Lady Dixie again pleads for justice for all the enslaved inhabitants of "erth" (the kingdom in which the play is set). The drama traces the history of a philosophical and physically powerful young woman, Isola, who is forced to marry the king of a neighboring state. A pantheist, who believes that nature is the "all Eternal, only God," Isola rejects artifical, man-made laws, including the "priestly exhortations" of a Church that makes laws for women whom it treats "as naught." [11] Defiantly, she proclaims that marriage has simply made her a "legal prostitute" and that she will not vow to obey her husband, "one who should be my equal and co-mate / But *not* my Lord and Master, I his slave" (7). In exposing the enslavement of women in a patriarchal society, the play traces its ancestry to feminist works like Mary Wollstonecraft's *A Vindication of the Rights of Woman* (1792). And with a revolutionary fervor that resembles Florence Nightingale's stirring call in *Cassandra*—"Awake, ye women, all ye that sleep awake"[12]—the play urges women to "rise from thy many thousand years of degradation," to repudiate the "superstition which enshrouds / Thy liberty," and to "cast off these cruel chains" (58).

Isola puts these words into action by deserting her husband and joining the revolutionary band that is fighting for the rights of another disinherited member of society, Vergli, her husband's illegitimate son by a common-law marriage. Because Vergli's mother has refused to endure the degrading wedding ceremony, her child is disinherited and disenfranchised. Vergli himself is a male Isola who espouses total equality of the sexes and classes, as well as improved living and working conditions, proportionate taxation, and vegetarianism. When he is captured and imprisoned, Isola, disguised as a man, rescues him; but she herself is taken, tried, and hanged. Her martyrdom, however, effects the social revolution she desired. A "Magna Charter of Human Rights" is passed, guaranteeing equality to all people, freedom of conscience in religion, the disestablishment of the Church, women's control over their own reproduction, and the right of the poor to live decently and eat well. The play closes with a Utopian vision of a world feminized and rendered Edenic, a world without bloodshed or war, without disease or hunger. In this newly constituted universe, sexual oppression is replaced by the "sweet companionship" of sexes "sharing in all things." Thus, a realignment of the relationship between the sexes is the essential first step in a social revolution. But the twenty-year-old wife and mother who envisioned this social reform could not herself become an Isola. Before she could emerge as a public militant, she had first to become a traveller, a voyager into other worlds that opened new possibilities for the female self.

Patagonia

Dixie's restless, iconoclastic energy, which had burst forth in *Isola,* could not be contained by domestic obligations nor released in social interactions. Feeling herself to be "palled for the moment with civilization and its surroundings . . . , weary of the shallow artificiality of modern existence," and longing for "a more vigorous emotion" than could be experienced in England,[13] Florence Dixie organized a party to travel to Patagonia, the largest desert in the Americas, located in the southern part of Argentina. Leaving behind her two small sons, Florence set forth on a six-month jaunt, in the company of "Beau," two of her brothers, and J. Beerbohm, a naturalist, a traveller, and the author of *Wanderings in Patagonia.*

Why Patagonia, of all the places on earth? As she explained in a humorous re-creation of a dialogue with astonished friends at the opening of her travel narrative, *Across Patagonia* (1880), this land allured her because it was so "outlandish and far away" and because it offered 100,000 unobstructed miles for riding, a healthy climate—that primary concern for so many nineteenth-century travellers—and freedom from "the persecutions of fevers, friends, savage tribes, obnoxious animals, telegrams, letters. . . ." More significantly, in such a land one could become a true adventurer, an explorer of "vast wilds, virgin as yet to the foot of man" (3). The spirit of Francis Douglas, who died scaling the Matterhorn for similar reasons, and of James Douglas, who perished on his pilgrimage to Palestine, lived on in Florence Douglas Dixie. Unlike either of these famous relatives, however, she survived her journey and recorded her adventures in a lively, popular travel book, *Across Patagonia,* which at least one reader found captivating: "I have done little," wrote the Duke of Somerset, "except . . . sit by the fire reading the travels of adventurous ladies . . . [like] Lady Florence Dixie who nearly starved in Patagonia."[14]

A rather conventional Victorian travel narrative, bearing few signs of the radical author of *Isola* in it, *Across Patagonia* begins predictably with a discussion of the motives for the journey and a catalogue of the equipment necessary for a jaunt to so remote a place. With only a few digressions on Argentinian history, culture, and geography, the book traces the travellers' progress from England to the "audacious" landscape of Rio, to "desolate and dreary" stretches of the Patagonian desert which seem "hardly of this world" (29), to the wild and spectacular Cordilleras of the Andes deep in Patagonia. The narrative not only limns the perilous adventures of their six-hundred-mile ride through uncivilized lands but also details the routine of daily life in the camps; it not only describes the exciting hunts for exotic game—guanaco, jaguars, ostriches—but also discusses, with a gourmet's relish, recipes for preparing the meat.

Neither the elaborate meals nor the spectacular landscapes make *Across Patagonia* lively reading; rather, the energetic, competent, sensitive narrative persona arrests readers' attention. With "masculine" hardihood, the narrator shoots, rides, and drinks with her male companions. With no hint of female squeamishness, she watches the disembowelment of the animals she has shot and rhapsodizes over the taste of their meat. She sleeps in the open air with her saddle for a pillow, bathes in icy streams, and contends with fires, storms, stampedes, and severe food shortages. After a day's ride she is "faint with hunger, drenched and cold; . . . so stiff that I could with difficulty move" (236) but uncomplaining. Unflinchingly, she endures a variety of injuries— falling down holes, being thrown from her mount—yet always she springs back into action. On one occasion the narrator even becomes a heroine. When the horses stampede, leaving the group stranded with no food, a distance of four days' walk from civilization, Lady Dixie singlehandedly finds the animals, improvises a bridle out of her scarf, and, riding bareback, drives the mounts to camp. Such exploits earned her a reputation as a woman with "powers of endurance equalled by few of either sex."[15]

But where in this hearty, buoyant book is *Isola*'s unconventional author? Although muted, her voice is heard in the poetic evocations of landscape, in the narrator's struggles with her feelings about hunting, and in her ambivalence about the Indians. At its best, Dixie's narrative captures the emotional tenor of the wild Patagonian landscape: the depressing effect of its barren plateaus, the eerieness of its ancient forests, with charred giant trees lying like "weird and ghastly" "skeletons of a bygone age" (193). Picturesque scenes abound. Looking over the silent camp with bodies stretched around the fire after a night of revelry, the narrator observes that "a few moonbeams struggled through the canopy of leaves . . . throwing strange lights and shadows; . . . the weird effect of the whole scene was heightened by the mysterious wail of the grebe . . . like the voice of an unquiet spirit" (51).

The narrator's own spirit is unquiet about hunting: the excitement of the chase thrills her, and her prose galvanizes when she describes a pursuit; yet, sensitive from childhood to the feelings of animals, Dixie is also repelled by hunting. She confesses that, though she and her party killed only for food and not for sport, she frequently "was haunted by a sad remorse for the loss of the innocent and trusting life" (182). Her affection for animals leads Dixie to adopt two South American pets: a dog, "Pucho," whose picture appears on the book's title page, and a jaguar, "Affums," whose appearance on a leash in London's parks caused a public sensation. Dixie recorded "Affums's" dramatic rescue from death and his subsequent career in Britain in an article in *Vanity Fair* (7 December 1881). The contest between her love for the aristocratic sport of hunting and her conscience was eventually resolved in favor of the latter, for in the 1880s Dixie joined the Humanitarian League and published a pamphlet on *The Horrors of Sport* (1895), indicting hunters for inflicting physical and psychological pain on animals and asserting that hunting is "barbarous" and pleasurable only to "a heart rendered callous by suffering often witnessed and little realized."[16]

Surprisingly, the author of *Isola* displays less sympathy for the people of Patagonia than she does for animals. Initially, she is content to make superficial judgments about "the natives" based solely on physical characteristics and rumor. Thus, she concludes that the inhabitants of Bahia de Todos los Santos must be happy because they are plump and chatter "like so many monkeys." The Indians of the desert interest her more, however, and she records their physical characteristics, dress, and behavior. Although annoyed by their unceremonious intrusions into her camp and their pilfering, Dixie is outraged by the way in which Indians are cheated by white people and horrified by their self-destructive behavior. The Tehuelch Indians, noted for their "easy-going good humor," are destroying all their other good qualities by the use of "aqua diente" (liquor) to which they are becoming addicted. Sadly, she predicts that "it is to be feared, they will become nothing more than a pack of impoverished, dirty, thieving raga-muffins" (69). This statement offers one of the few indications in *Across Patagonia* that Dixie took any interest in the fate of exploited South Americans. Yet, in only a year's time, she was to become a public advocate of another oppressed population—the Zulus of South Africa. Never again would she write a book with so little political import.

The War Correspondent, 1880–1881

While Patagonia did not awaken Florence Dixie's political conscience, it did nurture her wanderlust. Within a year of her return, she was already planning another escape from England—a journey to "the ice-bound land of North America . . . the crossing of the Behring Straits, and a winter's sojourn on the mystic Arctic shores of far-off Tuski-Land."[17] This time, however, pleasure alone did not seem to offer sufficient justification for travel. She therefore professed to have an ethnological motive for her journey: to study "the manners and customs" of the inhabitants of these "mystic shores." Clearly, her prodigious energy was seeking a more serious and professional outlet than that offered by travel for pleasure.

History conspired to provide her with just the opportunity she was seeking, but not in the Arctic wilds. In 1880 the tensions between the British and the Dutch settlers in southern Africa finally erupted into a war. In April 1877, the Administrator of the British colony of Natal, Theophilus Shepstone, had annexed the Afrikaner-controlled Transvaal in the name of the British Crown. Angered by Shepstone's inept administration and the "timorous despotism"[18] of his regime, the Boers rose against the British in December 1880, seizing control of Laing's Nek, a pass through the Drakensberg Mountains which gave access to the road to Natal. The initial battle of the First Anglo-Boer War was joined when the British unsuccessfully stormed these Boer entrenchments.

This war provided Lady Dixie with a new mission and a new role: she could emulate Florence Nightingale, who had made her name in the hospitals of the Crimea just a few years before Florence Douglas's birth. Characteristically, she imagined herself as going one step beynd her famous role model. Nightingale restricted herself to hospital nursing; Dixie would tend the wounded right on the field of battle: "In many cases the mortally stricken soldier is left to his last agony on the spot whereon he fell . . . and the one who might bring relief and tenderness to soothe his last moments is not always by. It was in this capacity that I decided to proceed at once to South Africa" (*LM,* 2).

In 1850 Florence Nightingale had felt that she had three careers among which she might choose: "a married woman, or a literary woman, or a hospital sister."[19] Florence Dixie, thirty years later, was offered the opportunity to embrace all three; Sir Algernon Borthwick, editor of the *Morning Post,* asked her to serve as the paper's special correspondent to cover the war. Her unique position as an aristocratic female war correspondent elicited some jealous remarks from papers like the *London Figaro:* "Society is considerably fluttered at the news that a real Baronet's wife is just off as a special correspondent. . . . The action of our contemporary in choosing not only a feminine 'special' but one with a handle on her name is most enterprising and spirited. . . , but it must not expect to be left alone in this particular respect. . . . Even now, we understand, overtures are being made to a Countess in her own right to proceed to the Transvaal . . . [and] an aristocratic contemporary of ours has hopes of securing a real dowager duchess to represent it at the seat of war." The article goes on to express a stern disapproval of the idea of a female special correspondent: "Male specials can be left to themselves, and must take the risks of war; but what embarrassment a pretty and titled feminine correspondent might be to a susceptible general. . . . We think that our feminine patricians should not lightly follow the example of the fair Amazon who will soon be in the Transvaal."[20]

But no backbiting could keep the "fair Amazon" from the scene of the action. Embarking with her husband and a servant on the *Warwick Castle,* she sailed into Cape Town on Friday, 11 March 1881. Her delight at the termination of a tedious voyage was clouded by the shocking news that the British forces had been defeated for the third time in the war at a battle on the Majuba Mountain. Sir George Colley, High Commissioner for Southeastern Africa and commander of the troops, had been killed in action. Still reeling from the blow to their "British arrogance" (*LM,* 7), the Dixies spent a subdued four days sight-seeing in Cape Town. For Lady Dixie, one of the primary "sights" was the captive Zulu king Cetshwayo. Her visit to the barren farmhouse on the outskirts of Cape Town where he was imprisoned was to provide a new direction to both her travels and the next year of her life.

Cetshwayo had been officially crowned by Theophilus Shepstone in 1877 as a sign of the alliance between the British and the Zulu against their common foe, the Boers. However, after England annexed the Transvaal, the Boers came under British hegemony and their disputes with the Zulus threatened the peace and security of a British colony. The authorities in the Transvaal responded by finding fault with Cetshwayo: he was cruel, he persecuted Christian converts, his *impi* (warriors) violated the border between Zululand and Natal, he was strengthening his military machine for war. After presenting Cetshwayo with a politically unrealistic ultimatum, the British invaded Zululand in January 1879. Although they suffered several stunning defeats administered by the disciplined, brave Zulu warriors, the British finally routed Cetshwayo's troops, deposed the king himself, and divided Zululand among thirteen rival chiefs in a "Machiavellian" strategy[21] designed to prevent the resurgence of the Zulu nation.

The exiled, imprisoned Cetshwayo, whom Lady Dixie met, was a plump, congenial man with a "pleasing and kindly countenance" and a "nobility of soul"; in no way did he resemble the "ignorant and bloodthirsty despot"[22] depicted in the war propaganda. This man, whom she described in her *Morning Post* despatches as "every inch a king,"[23] awakened Dixie's aristocratic sympathies; moreover, he touched a deep chord in her that had sounded in early works like *Isola* and the childhood poems—a passionate opposition to injustice and an identification with all the "dispossessed" of the earth. Therefore, when this stranger urged Dixie to visit his land and investigate the attitude of his people toward the British settlement, she agreed. The fulfillment of this promise was to involve her in a public crusade and to have a lasting influence on her life.

Almost immediately after this momentous interview, the Dixies began their journey to the war front by sailing to Durban, a port in Natal. The details of their wanderings across South Africa are recorded in Florence Dixie's despatches to the *Morning Post,* published between April and November of 1881, and in the narrative of her travels, *In the Land of Misfortune* (1882).

The journey to the war front resembled a holiday outing: at Durban the Dixies were feted by the Army, at Pietermaritzburg they bought horses and went sight-seeing. But at Estcourt they were greeted by the disconcerting and "shocking" news that the British had signed a peace agreement with the victorious Boers. A war correspondent with no war, Lady Dixie reverted for a time to the familiar pattern of Patagonian travel, becoming a peripatetic hunter and observer of life. Joining the 58th regiment to which her cousin was attached, Florence Dixie hunted, rode, entertained officers (with her husband serving as cook), and travelled with the Army, sleeping out under the stars when hotels were too dirty or too full of drunken Boers to be habitable. She toured the battlefields of the late war, calling to mind friends who had died. When Sir Evelyn Wood marched the Army across the Transvaal in a symbolic show of force, the Dixies went along, observing on the way the anger of the British settlers at their government's "betrayal" of them to the Boers. In the *Morning Post* (2 April 1882), Dixie quotes the *Natal Mercury:* "Once more is the Transvaal to be given up to the license and liberty of Boer mismanagement and evil rule." At Pretoria, the capital of the Transvaal, Florence Dixie got her first taste of the world of politics into which she would soon eagerly plunge herself. The Royal Commission on the future of the Transvaal was meeting in the house where the Dixies were staying. As the Afrikaner leaders, Jan Brand and Piet Joubert, argued out a settlement with British officials, Lady Dixie sat—with open ears—under the conference room windows. A nationalistic Briton, she was angered by her country's concessions to the Boers, but she also began to realize Britain's "fickleness" in its dealings with Africans. A deputation of African chiefs confronted Sir Evelyn Wood with their fears that the return of the Transvaal to the Boers would mean war between black and white. Horrified, Dixie watched Wood placate them with empty promises of British assistance against the Boers in such a case.

An arduous return journey brought the Dixies back to their original camp by 4 July. Immediately, Lady Dixie began planning her trip to Zululand; however, unrest in that territory, resulting from the rivalry of two chiefs, forced her to abandon this excursion temporarily. Soon bored with the routine of Army camp life, the Dixies decided to strike out on their own for Kimberley, the boomtown which had grown up around the diamond mines. Reaching there entailed some of the roughest and most dangerous travelling yet; tossed about like mail sacks on rickety carts and at the mercy of drunken or careless guides, the Dixies twice narrowly missed serious injury or death. Once, Florence Dixie woke in time to prevent the cart from plunging into a twenty-foot chasm; on another day, the horses, out of control, raced down a precipitous mountain pass and the carriage careened into a ditch, falling on top of Florence herself, who was uninjured but shaken by the accident.

The goal of this difficult journey was a "vast, straggling town," which offered the tourist only a hospital, a prison, and the famed diamond mines—all disturbing or depressing places. A hot, dirty place, critically understaffed, the hospital was filled with Africans lying helpless on mattresses on the ground "where cold draughts swept over them night and day (*LM,* 280). Lady Dixie was appalled to see a quadruple amputee "eking out the last few hours of life" in that "den of misery" with no one by to help him slake his thirst (*LM*, 282). Unlike Florence Nightingale, however, Florence Dixie did not stay to tend this sufferer or to reform the "disgraceful" hospital administration; she simply dispensed some private charity and fled to more cheerful places.

Although hardly more cheerful, the diamond mines did offer Dixie food for thought. Anthony Trollope, looking into these pits in the mid-1870s, had seen the toiling of Africans as "growing Christians,"[24] but this lady traveller instead saw budding revolutionaries, who, while "fashioning out of the pit [diamonds] . . . to bring gain to the white man, forgot not the future for which they lent their toil. . . . They too could look ahead and dream of Eldorado—for was not the money gained by such toil quickly to be converted into arms, ammunition . . . to wrest back . . . their own fair land" (*LM*, 279–80).

The nascent sympathy that Dixie here expresses for the exploited Africans comes to fruition in the next and final stage of her adventures—the journey to Zululand. When the Dixies returned to the Army camp near Newcastle, they discovered that Sir Evelyn Wood was about to march into Zululand for a meeting with the chiefs at Inhslazatye to assess the success of the British partition of Zululand. Florence Dixie would finally be able to fulfill her promise to Cetshwayo. The mud, the heat, the repeated wagon accidents, and the interminable delays made the march to Zululand like others the Dixies had taken with the Army; however, Florence Dixie's experiences in Zululand were unique in their psychological impact. Visiting the sites of famous battles of the Zulu war, Dixie was thrilled at the thought that 26,000 Zulu warriors had risen to defend their "dearly loved land" (*LM*, 328) against the British invaders. At the Inhslazatye meeting, she witnessed with outrage the silencing of those chiefs loyal to Cetshwayo who attempted to advocate his reinstatement. When Dixie herself tried to inquire from a group of Zulus how they felt about the king's restoration, the army translator was not allowed to transmit the question. Determined to find her own answers, Florence Dixie separated herself, physically and symbolically as well, from the Army and, after a visit to Cetshwayo's capital of Ulundi, set out to survey the opinion of the Zulu people about the existing political tensions in Zululand and the restoration of their king. Two weeks of travelling convinced her of what she already knew in her heart: there was "a universal desire on the part of the Zulu nation for their king's return" (*MP*, 1 November 1881).

Armed with this conviction, Florence returned to Pietermaritzburg in September 1881, where she met the notorious John Colenso, the Bishop of Natal whose controversial biblical scholarship had called into question the historical accuracy of the Pentateuch. A scholar of the Zulu language and culture, Colenso, whom the Zulu affectionately called "Sobantu" or "Father of the People," supported Cetshwayo's cause. Despite their religious differences, the agnostic Dixie and the unorthodox Bishop agreed on the issue of the Zulu king. Just as Dixie was delighted to have found an ally, especially one well-acquainted with the Zulus and the history of the king's case, the Bishop was happy to have discovered an aristocratic campaigner for Cetshwayo. Colenso wrote to his son Francis in England: "Lady F. D. will be a strong help to us with the Conservative Party to which she belongs."[25]

Returning to Cape Town in mid-September, the Dixies were caught up in the social whirl of civilized life. Lady Dixie's thoughts were not on balls or social calls, however, but on the fate of the king whose passionate advocate she had become. Within a few days, she visited Cetshwayo who, to her eyes, had aged sadly since her previous visit. After recounting her journey and expressing her conviction that the Zulu wanted their king back, Dixie discussed with Cetshwayo his projected visit to England to place his case for restoration to power before British officials. Dixie promised the king "not to forget or forsake" his cause. In the course of her journey she had clearly undergone a metamorphosis: after her initial visit, Dixie had written to the *Morning Post,* urging that Cetshwayo be released from prison and allowed to visit his homeland; after this second visit, she advocated his restoration to full kingly power in a reunited Zululand.

Clearly, as this brief summary of her travels indicates, Florence Dixie's journey across South Africa was not only a physical but a psychological odyssey. The traveller who returned to Cape Town after six exhausting months on the road had awakened to a new perception of Britain's injustice to Africans. Through a series of eye-opening experiences—the official treatment of the black deputation at Pretoria, the sufferings of Africans in the Transvaal, the unrest among Zulus caused by the British partition of Zululand, and the meeting at Inhslazatye—Dixie came to sympathize with the African people. The turning point of Dixie's inner journey took place in Zululand—from then on Cetshwayo's cause was her own. When she pledged herself to the king in that bare farmhouse outside Cape Town, she was embarking on a campaign that would absorb a year of her time as well as a vast amount of her energy and would transform a dilettantish lady traveller into a public champion of justice—for the Zulu, for the Irish, for animals, and for women, too.

Champion of the Zulu

Even before she sailed from South Africa, Dixie had begun her political campaigning: she sent the *Morning Post* an account of her final interview with Cetshwayo, adding at the end a plea for his restoration to power. Published soon after her arrival in England, this article precipitated a reply from Lord Chelmsford, Commander-in-Chief of the British forces in South Africa during the Zulu War. In a letter to the editor of the *Morning Post* (2 November 1881), Chelmsford accused Dixie of speaking from a "purely sentimental point of view" and of being either "imperfectly acquainted with" or "wilfully" ignorant of the facts. Although he admitted that the British settlement in Zululand had been a failure, Chelmsford argued that Cetshwayo's restoration would reintroduce the threat of a united Zulu nation and would thus jeopardize the residents of Natal and the Transvaal. But Florence Dixie was not about to be bullied by charges of sentimentality or insufficient evidence. With the help of the Colenso family, she began to deluge the press with letters and articles detailing the history of the Zulu War, the sociology of Zulu tribes, and the duplicitous behavior of the British. The *Morning Post* (7 November 1881) published her extensive letter, "Cetshwayo: An Inquiry and Defence," and its editor issued a laudatory statement about Dixie's work for the paper. Commending her "justness of observation" and the vivid accuracy of description in her despatches, the editorial praised her for "the distances which have been traversed, the difficult situations which have been met with equal courage and composure [that] would do credit to any of the war correspondents of the English Press." On 12 November 1881, *Vanity Fair* issued a statement favorable to Cetshwayo's reinstatement and then, between 10 December 1881 and 4 February 1882, published a series of nine meticulously detailed articles written by Florence Dixie and entitled *A Defence of Zululand and Its King: echoes from the Blue Books*. These articles were collected and published as a book in April 1882, with an appendix containing the extensive correspondence about Cetshwayo in the pages of the *Morning Post*. Chelmsford could not fault these articles for ignorance of facts, for they bristle with quotations from government documents which show Britain's unjust treatment of the Zulu.

The pamphlet begins by citing Zulu grievances against the Boers because of their encroachments on Zulus' land and against the British because of their refusal to acknowledge the decision of a Boundary Commission (appointed by the Governor of Natal) when that body found in favor of the Zulu. It then addresses, one by one, the charges against Cetshwayo's regime that had been cited as the causes of the invasion: the putative military buildup along the border with the Transvaal, Cetshwayo's alleged brutality toward missionaries and his own people, his failure to live up to coronation promises, and Zulu incursions into British territory, particularly the nororious Sihayo raid. In each of these instances Cetshwayo is shown to be a wronged man, a just ruler who had been "played with and baffled by" the British for more than sixteen years (*Defence*, 14). Thus, although the author denies that Cetshwayo was massing his forces for an attack on the British in 1879, she argues that, if he had done so, the king would have been entirely within his rights. The tales of his savage butchery of his own people, particularly Christian converts, and his persecution of missionaries, Dixie dismisses as "nothing but a tissue of inventions and exaggerations" (*Defence*, 21). She challenges

Cetshwayo's detractors to provide hard evidence of his atrocities, and herself produces proof that only three Christians were killed during Cetshwayo's reign—two of those not for religious reasons but for infractions of Zulu law. No sympathizer with missionaries herself, Dixie demonstrates that Cetshwayo, who never persecuted or expelled one of them, showed remarkable tolerance for missionaries who often caused social disruption in his kingdom.

In her discussion of the Zulu king's alleged brutality, Dixie betrays an interesting cultural relativism analogous to that of Mary Kingsley in her defense of cannibalism among the tribes of West Africa. Lady Dixie defends the Zulus' rights to abide by tribal traditions, even those involving practices she finds personally repulsive; she is adamant that the British have no right to impose their laws on the Zulu people. Although she condones Britain's interference in the Transvaal, she condemns her country's attempt to meddle in Zulu affairs. At times, the feminist Dixie finds herself in the anomalous position of having to defend the Zulu treatment of women as, for example, in the so-called Sihayo raid. Two wives of the Zulu chief Sihayo had taken lovers during their husband's absence; to avenge the family honor, a party of Sihayo's sons and relatives had attacked the culprits, all of whom fled across the border into Natal. They were pursued, the women taken and forcibly returned to Zululand, where they were executed. Although, in the past, British authorities had allowed Zulus to try their own people, even for offenses committed in British territory, the Sihayo raid was treated differently by a government looking for a justification for war. The authorities demanded that the raiders be returned to Natal for trial by British law and that a large fine be paid as compensation. As Dixie points out, Cetshwayo was puzzled by the attention this incident received and the importance it was accorded in the ultimatum sent to him by Sir Bartle Frere. To Dixie it seemed clear that the British government was fabricating excuses for an invasion of Zululand.

Strangely, Florence Dixie's analysis of the Sihayo raid manifests none of the feminist anger that had characterized her earlier writing; she refrains from criticizing the Zulu for behavior that she would have found reprehensible in Britain. It seems as if, for a time, Cetshwayo's cause eclipsed and even subsumed all others; into it, she poured all her rage at social injustice. Dixie may have sensed the contradictions inherent in her position, for she even tried to shift some of the blame for the Zulu treatment of women onto the shoulders of the British by asserting that their practice of returning to Zululand females who had fled to Natal for refuge encouraged the Zulu to see women as property (*Defence*, 40). In addition, she acerbically reminded her readers that the supposed atrocities of Cetshwayo were nothing in comparison to the extermination by the "civilized" inhabitants of Europe of women accused of witchcraft. Dixie's refusal to judge Zulus by absolute and traditional moral standards led her detractors to accuse her of having forgotten the distinction between right and wrong. Rider Haggard, for instance, sneered that the arguments of the "lady advocates" of the Zulu king "bear about the same resemblance to the truth . . . [as] the speech to the jury by the council for the defense in a hopeless murder trial."[26]

Haggard's jibe does pinpoint an essential quality of *A Defence of Zululand:* despite its eighty-odd pages of minute fact and its ponderous title, the work is not a flatly factual, dry, emotionless political tract. Instead, it is an impassioned personal plea for justice for a wronged man. The emotional tone of the piece is set in the opening paragraph: "In a lonely and dreary captivity we are keeping this king who never harmed us, who never menaced us, who honestly and anxiously desired to live in peace with the people to whom his feelings and interests told him to be friendly" (1). The intensity of Dixie's concern for this "lonely and helpless captive" (78), whom she had met only a few times before she became his champion, seems puzzling in light of the fact that she displayed little sympathy for the inhabitants of South America during her journey there. What was there about the Zulu king and the Zulu people that so fired her imagination? The answer lies partly in the prevailing mythology about the Zulu nation and partly in Dixie's own emotional development in adolescence.

As Dorothy Hammond and Alta Jablow observe in *The Myth of Africa,* at the end of the eighteenth century, the European imagination often depicted Africa as an Arcadia inhabited by noble savages.[27] One of the first examples of such mythologizing appeared in one of the earliest novels by a woman, Aphra Behn's *Oronooko; or, The Royal Slave* (1688). The hero of this work is a handsome, aristocratic, Caucasian-looking (he even has a "Roman" nose) West African prince who has been made a slave in Surinam. Kept alive by the antislavery forces in the early nineteenth century, this tradition of the noble savage also manifested itself in the "novels of empire," written in the 1880s and 1890s, through the idealization of the Zulus. Because of their pleasing looks, their legendary bravery, and their Spartan social organization, the Zulus captured the romantic side of the European imagination. As a result, even so proper a British lady as Mrs. Wilkinson, the wife of a missionary to Zululand in the 1870s, confessed that she found Cetshwayo to be a "fine, tall handsome man"[28] and the Zulus to be "so handsome and so well made, it is a pleasure to look at them."[29] Rider Haggard intimated that Florence Dixie's sympathy for Cetshwayo was based chiefly on his looks: "Lady Florence Dixie waves his banner and informs the public through the columns of the newspapers how good, how big, and how beautiful he is."[30]

To many Europeans Zulus seemed to be natural aristocrats whose stately and dignified bearing set them apart from other Africans. To some, they resembled the brave (but barely civilized) ancestors of the British people. An arresting example of this imaginative identification of the Zulu and the Norseman occurs in Rider Haggard's classic adventure novel, *King Solomon's Mines* (1885). At a climactic point in the novel, Twala, the brutal king of a people who resemble the Zulu, joins in hand-to-hand combat with an English traveller, Sir Henry Curtis. As he prepares for battle, Sir Henry metamorphoses into one of his long-haired Nordic forebears. As the opponents face each other with raised axes, the narrator comments: "For a moment, they stood thus, and the setting sun caught their stalwart frames and clothed them both in fire. They were a well-matched pair."[31] Interestingly, the editor of the *Morning Post,* in an editorial supporting Cetshwayo's restoration to power, draws a similar comparison; the Zulus, he asserts, resemble the loyal Scottish supporters of Bonnie Prince Charlie, the young Pretender to the throne: "The Zulu braves are dusky Jacobites, and it is the King who was carried away in a big ship 'over the water' who still occupies the hearts of wild Highlanders and Lowlanders beside the White and the Black Umvolosi" (7 November 1881). It is easy to see how Florence Douglas Dixie, with the blood of patriotic Scotsmen in her veins, would join in this romanticization of the Zulu people.

The courage of Zulus both in legend and in actuality also captured the imaginations of European writers. After all, despite the fact that they lost the war, the Zulus had scored a tremendous victory over the British at Isandhlwana (1879) where 1,600 of Her Majesty's troops had been killed. This tribe was perceived to be a "worthy foe," an opponent whose values—loyalty and bravery—made them the savage soul mates of the British.[32] Dixie argued that "the noble savage can appreciate courage as well as, ay and better than, the white man of civilization" (*LM*, 361). Repeatedly, she depicted Zulus in terms with which the British audience could identify, as in this passage from *In the Land of Misfortune:* "Those 26,000 warriors of Cetshwayo . . . for king and country came to strike a blow at the invaders of their dearly loved land. What to them was death? They feared it not. . . . Yet it was a noble foe against whom the English fought that day" (329). Similarly, in limning the sorrows of the deposed, suffering Zulu monarch, she was presenting a picture with which any loyal inhabitant of a monarchy could sympathize.

But the popular idealizations of the Zulu and their similarities to the Scots or the English cannot fully explain Dixie's personal commitment to Cetshwayo, nor can these account for her characterization of the king as a tragic hero. When Dixie wrote for the *Morning Post* (1 November 1881) her narrative of the final interview with Cetshwayo, she depicted him as a tragic figure given to poetic lamentations: "All I love is in Zululand; my heart is there, where lies my father's grave. I am heart-sick and weary with waiting. When will England be just and let me return? Do you think that because I am a black man, I cannot feel, or suffer the less by this long, long, and weary captivity?" Cetshwayo's message to the English people is also delivered "with grave dignity" and is phrased in elegantly cadenced prose: "Tell them that I am a king and a captive; that I am alone and helpless; that I am very sad and heartbroken. . . . Ask them to be my friend, and to help me. I have no more to say." Although Dixie claims to have "faithfully" reproduced the king's speech, it seems likely that those eloquent words have had their poetic value enhanced by the recording hand.

In a real sense, then, the drama of Cetshwayo's life reifies the drama that Dixie's imagination had shaped just a few years before in *Isola*. Cetshwayo, like the women and Vergli in that early play, is a disinherited creature; John Dunn, the "white Zulu" betrayer of Cetshwayo who now held power in Zululand, where he kept a "harem" and flouted "the laws of civilization" (*LM*, 424), is the evil exemplar of patriarchy. Deprived of his rightful property and exiled from his own people by the actions of Britain, Cetshwayo, in Dixie's mind, serves as an imaginative analogue of the British woman, whose property is not her own after marriage and whose children are not legally hers. (The Second Married Woman's Property Act was only passed in 1882 and the Infant Act in 1886.) Cetshwayo is a victim of the "ambition and cupidity of others" (*LM*, 11); like women he is powerless before the might of white, patriarchal, imperialistic Britain. Furthermore, like economically and politically impotent Victorian women, Cetshwayo, imprisoned in a small, barren house, has been stripped of both independence and identity. Later in her life Dixie was to make this implicit parallel even more obvious when she told the Women's Franchise League that women were slaves of their husbands, prisoners of a restrictive social and legal system, and powerless creatures who could not even claim their bodies as their own. It would seem, then, that Cetshwayo's plight unleashed a whole set of subconscious associations in Dixie's mind and that she channeled into his cause a reservoir of repressed anger and energy. The writer of *Isola* surfaces again in the passionate polemicist of *The Defence of Zululand and Its King*.

Florence Dixie's sense of personal identification with the king may have been responsible for some of the tactical errors that she made in her campaign. Always impulsive, she seems to have acted with a particular lack of restraint on at least one occasion. Cetshwayo had sent her letters for both the Queen and the Prince Consort, which Dixie had not only passed along through proper channels but had also sent to the *Morning Post* for publication. In addition, she published a personal letter from Cetshwayo into which she interpolated some sentences from an earlier letter— these sentences unleashed a controversy that led to the post- ponement of Cetshwayo's visit to England. He had been fortunate enough to have as an interpreter a sympathetic friend, Mr. Sam- uelson, the son of some missionaries. When the trip to England was being negotiated, British authorities replaced Samuelson with Henriques Shepstone, son of Theophilus Shepstone, the retired Administrator of the Transvaal. Dixie was suspicious of Shep- stone's political views and was led to believe by a letter that Cetshwayo, too, was upset at his appointment: "I hear that one I cannot trust is to be my interpreter to England . . . . Why is my present interpreter taken from me?"[33] When Dixie inserted these sentences into Cetshwayo's letter in the *Morning Post,* British officials got angry, the Shepstone family (who had now secretly switched their support to Cetshwayo) got angrier, and both Sam- uelson and Cetshwayo denied that the interpolated sentences were the king's. Samuelson was dismissed as the interpreter and Dixie was left frustrated and embarrassed, able to conclude only that the original letter containing the offending sentences must have been a forgery designed to discredit her and the king. She de- manded that the correspondence be published by the Colonial Office and begged to be allowed to take full responsibility for the incident.

After this diplomatic contretemps, the months passed, frus- tration mounted, but still Cetshwayo was not allowed to come to England to confer about his future. In May there was a rising in Zululand that gave urgency to the case. Lady Dixie seems to have been in the middle of the action, for she wrote in the *Nineteenth Century*[34] that, learning from private sources of the imminence of such an uprising, she "despatched a messenger to Zululand to stay the rising and if possible avert hostilities."

Finally, thirteen months after Florence Dixie had left him at Oude Molen, Cetshwayo arrived in England in August 1882 for two months of meetings with the Queen, the Colonial Office, and a curious public. Dixie's involvement in Cetshwayo's fortunes was humorously celebrated by the *St. James Gazette,* which depicted her as:

> The lady in command
> Of the happy transformation—
> Zulu, into Dixie's Land. (3 July 1882)

During the spring and summer, as these negotiations for Cetshwayo's trip were inching forward, Florence was busy writing *In the Land of Misfortune,* the book that would detail her transformation into his public advocate.

In the Land of Misfortune

As its title suggests, Dixie's second travel book, published in November 1882, aims to be far more than four hundred pages of entertaining narrative incorporating some of the material from her columns for the *Morning Post.* It is in many ways a conventional travel book, which begins with the persona's reasons for embarking and traces her progress through Africa in a chronologically ordered narrative, blending description of scenery and modes of travel with personal observation on a variety of subjects. But it is, in addition, a book designed to educate its readers about two political "misfortunes" for which Britain has been responsible in South Africa—the destruction of the Zulu nation and the surrender of the Transvaal to Afrikaner control as a result of the Pretoria Convention of 1881. As a vehicle of anti-Boer propaganda, the book was published almost a year too late, but as a paean to Cetshwayo and to the Zulu people it was more timely, for it appeared within months of Cetshwayo's successful visit to England during which he became a celebrity: photographed in European clothes, mobbed on the streets of London, and even caricatured in *Punch.* When Cetshwayo departed for Africa, his restoration to power was virtually assured, but the extent of that power was still being debated by the Colonial Office in the autumn of 1882 when Dixie's book appeared. Her work, then, had the virtue of keeping the king and his claims before the public eye. Indeed, the narrative is structured in such a way— beginning and ending in vividly dramatic interviews with the imprisoned king—as to make him seem like the presiding spirit of Dixie's whole journey. Thus, her eventual visit to Zululand and return to Cetshwayo seem, in the context of the work, the inevitable fulfillment of a pattern implicit in the action from the beginning.

Dixie also punctuates the narrative of her travels with reminders of the other "misfortune" she witnessed, the British conduct of the First Anglo-Boer War. Whenever she visited the battlefields of that conflict—as she often did as a war correspondent travelling with the Army—Dixie used that opportunity not only to indulge in some verbal landscape painting but also to celebrate the bravery of the British and to denigrate the military prowess of the Boers. Her battlefield pieces always return to the same point—the heroic sacrifices of British troops were in vain because the government capitulated too soon and too easily. For example, while visiting Laing's Nek, the site of the first engagement of the war, she reflects that the British attack on the Boer mountain stronghold was folly comparable to that of the infamous charge of the 600 in the Crimea: "In the many valuable lives so uselessly thrown away we mourn the loss of . . . men, who, we cannot help but feel, were sacrificed in a hopeless cause, and died, alas! in vain" (*LM*, 55). She also makes her political points through the narrative of her journey across the Transvaal to Potchefstroom, where the British settlers had withstood a painful siege during the war. By recording sympathetically the settlers' hostility to a government that seems to have betrayed them, Dixie is in effect making a political argument. She tells us that in the Transvaal "disgust and contempt had asserted their reign, and the minds of the settlers harboured all that was bitter and unforgiving toward the authors of a policy which they asserted would be their ruin" (*LM*, 159).

Also highly political is the portrayal of the Boers she encountered in the Transvaal and the Orange Free State. Dixie's anger at their "undeserved" victory over England and her personal distaste for their life style and values emerge in the unrelentingly negative pictures that she draws of the Boers. Almost without exception they are presented as surly, dirty, grossly fat, and drunken creatures. Dixie's depiction of Cronje (the man who had led the siege of Potchefstroom) gives evidence of her prejudices. Noticing him in front of a "dirty and greasy-looking tent," she comments:

It was with some curiosity that I looked at the man whose behavior to dying women and children shut up in that fort during the siege must ever reflect shame on himself. . . . It was a pleasanter face to look at than I had pictured to myself; but his eyes had a bad expression, and the cunning cruel look in them overbalanced any other redeeming points. (LM, 149)

An advocate of family planning, Dixie disapproved of the Boers' excessive breeding; moreover, she was angered by their inhospitality to British travellers. For example, after she was grudgingly received into a farmhouse for a night's lodging, Dixie comtemplated the supper offered her with revulsion: "A plate of fat was placed in front of me, a piece of bread and a cup of tea. There was no salt forthcoming to make the fat palatable, and sugar was a thing unknown" (LM, 298). Louisa Hutchinson, Florence Dixie, and a number of other women travellers in the second half of the nineteenth century drew similar pictures of the Boers. For example, Emma Rutherford Murray, who travelled across South Africa in 1856–60, noted the "multiplicity of children . . . ten or twelve children is the ordinary number in a Boer family" and commented with a certain nationalistic pique: "I wonder the Dutch race has not swallowed up the land."[35] The American Louise Vescelles-Sheldon was also offended by the dirt and the bad, expensive food of the Boers; moreover, she found the Boer women to be "immense."[36] Finally, Mrs. Lionel Phillips disapprovingly described a Boer family outside Johannesburg which consisted of "the farmer and his wife, several married sons and daughters and their numerous progeny all in the most hopeless state of dirt and stolidity."[37] Occasionally, Dixie herself humorously dramatizes the stolidity of the Boers: having arrived at a farmhouse and passed through the mandatory, extended handshaking ritual, she describes herself as "relaps[ing] into a statue" like the rest of the company, who sit in complete silence for an hour and then solemnly shake hands again (*LM*, 296).

Although British chauvinism undoubtedly produced some of her hostility to the Boers, Lady Dixie had several unpleasant encounters that intensified her animosity toward the Dutch farmers. Twice farmers sold her dying horses at high prices, and once she was actually driven off a farm where she sought rest and food for her horses. She was also appalled by the Boers' treatment of Africans. Like H. Rider Haggard, who accused the Boers of believing that "they were entrusted by the Almighty with the task of exterminating the heathen native tribes around them,"[38] Dixie angrily censured what she perceived as Boer hypocrisy: "With the Bible in one hand, the Boer breathes prayer and cant while with the other he oppresses the black man" (*MP*, 28 July 1881).

Although she witnessed no large-scale oppression, she did observe, individual acts of cruelty toward Africans. One evening she discovered a "poor, half naked" African, huddling and shivering in a wagon while his master drank inside the warm hotel. Incensed by his needless suffering, Dixie ordered blankets and a hot drink, and forcibly restrained his drunken master from leaving before they arrived. When the master called the African a "dog," she retorted: "I don't know what you call a dog; if he is one . . . he is a much nicer creature than you are" (*LM*, 246). Clearly, to be sympathetic to the plight of Africans in the nineteenth century was almost invariably to be anti-Boer.[39] Yet none of the women travellers who criticize the Boers seems to be aware of her own cultural biases or the valid reasons for the Boers' hostility to the British. It remained for the South African novelist Olive Schreiner to present the Afrikaner perception of the British through the words of Tant' Sannie in *Story of an African Farm:* "Dear Lord! . . . . all Englishmen are ugly."[40]

But the anti-Boer propaganda never interferes with the lively narrative of *In the Land of Misfortune,* which encompasses both the exciting physical action and the verbal scene-painting necessary to a popular travel book. The *Athenaeum* praised the book's immediacy and the "unconventional freedom" of its style, which enables a reader "to picture to himself more vividly than he could otherwise do what it is like to live in the veldt."[41] Although Dixie does often describe the colors and textures of the African landscape, she seldom provides any scientific data about the climate, geology, flora, or fauna of Africa in this book, which, ironically, is dedicated to that great scientific traveller Charles Darwin. Instead, landscape is presented in terms of its psychological effect on the viewer or its political significance. For example, while visiting Ulundi, Cetshwayo's capital and the site of a bloody battle in the Zulu War, Dixie observes "large heaps of skeletons" strewing the field; to her these bones tell "a silent tale of bravery of a vanquished nation": "the verdant basin, the green emerald hills, the golden sun lighting up the trophies of nature's abundance; and then, through the dancing gleams of sunlight . . . the vast black circles which show where ruin reigns, and the ghastly grinning emblems of death mocking, as it were, at mercy, justice, and fair-play" (*LM,* 391–93). The traveller's imagination juxtaposes light and dark, life and death, to create a picturesque scene, emblematic of Britain's hypocrisy and injustice.

When Dixie looks at a glorious natural scene, she responds to its poetic effects. When she looks at a Zulu, she sees a man or woman who has been wrongly used—not the subject of scientific or scholarly study. Although committed to the reunification of the Zulu nation under Cetshwayo, Dixie is by no means a student of Zulu culture: readers learn little about the social structure, religion, or customs of the nation she is trying to reunite. Equally unscientific is her approach to the exotic animals of Africa, which she sees with a hunter's, not a zoologist's, eyes. Stalking a wild creature, Dixie may note its unique physical characteristics, but the drama of the chase is her primary interest. The other creatures she encounters on her travels—dogs, horses, trek oxen, mules—

are lovingly and sympathetically described, and their "rights" are defended against human beings who would abuse them. In fact, animals often become more vivid characters than people: her dog and her ponies, Punch and Nancy, for example, upstage her travelling companions and even her husband. Such sympathy for dumb beasts could not help but move a Victorian audience that admired the paintings of an Edwin Landseer and could not help but convince it of the reliability and decency of the book's narrator.

But the narrator of *In the Land of Misfortune* is not only compassionate, she is also a vigorous, cool, competent woman who is as tough as the men in her party. Always the first to awaken, she paces her male companions in their riding, hunting, or climbing during the day. When in pain, she stoically refuses to inflict her sufferings on others: "I was undergoing an agony of thirst, and my tongue . . . had withered up and clung to the roof of my mouth . . . my feet began to swell. . . . These little annoyances, I, however, kept to myself, for fear of being a nuisance" (*LM,* 346–47). In understated tones she dismisses several potentially serious physical injuries. Having tumbled into a mountain chasm while climbing alone, she calmly admires the beauty of the spot and then extricates herself by climbing a trailing vine. When a carriage overturns on top of her and she is "crushed by a heavy weight," Dixie stoically resigns herself to the feeling "of the inevitable, which those who have faced death and given up all hope know so well" (*LM,* 303). This cool detachment in the face of danger makes her scornful of typically "feminine" responses to peril. As the Dixies cling desperately to the side of a carriage that is careening out of control down a steep slope, she pauses to laugh at a group of young ladies in the coach who are screaming in chorus like "a lot of hungry pigs" (*LM,* 256). When action is required, however, Lady Dixie seizes the moment—snatching the reins from the hands of the driver of their cart and galloping down the road before they are trapped in a bandit's ambush. Gleefully, she narrates the termination of this dramatic episode: "An hour before the appointed time the inhabitants of Winburg were surprised by the arrival of Her Majesty's mail cart, which, driven by a lady, might have been seen entering the town" (*LM*, 271). The unconventional woman who enjoyed challenging traditional ideas about her sex obviously relished this role reversal.

In fact, throughout the narrative, Dixie creates a comic subplot based on the role reversals in her domestic life. In this comedy, Sir Alexander Beaumont Dixie is almost always asleep and unwilling to be awakened; his wife is thus compelled to assume an assertive role in her attempts to rouse him. Sometimes bedbugs serve as allies in her mock-heroic campaign; at other times, she must adopt direct measures like "striking the tent in which he lay" (*LM*, 115). Her husband's "stolid indifference" to all noise when he is asleep produces some humorous consequences. Marauding mules invade the Dixies' tent and steal food before Lady Dixie awakens and chases them across camp to recover the pilfered supplies. When the disgruntled wife returns to the tent, she is greeted by a drowsy "What's the matter?", to which she rather shrewishly responds: "If every Zulu in Zululand were in this tent all assegaing [spearing] you at once, you would sleep through it all." Then, with a mockery of her own wifely exaggerations, she adds: "Certainly, the tent would have been a miraculous one to have held several thousand men; while the unfortunate victim . . . would undoubtedly have slept on with a vengeance!" (*LM*, 373). The narrator thus manages to laugh not only at her husband's behavior but at her own rather absurd overreaction to his somnolence.

The narrator uses this same double-edged mockery in describing her husband's dismay at the repulsive fare at an Afrikaner farm: "Being hungry . . . I bolted my food, the while indulging in covert glances of amusement at my husband's face of silent despair. To think that he should be reduced after all, to drinking tea, and to see him actually swallowing it, was almost too ludicrous. I fairly laughed outright, which at once drew upon me the astonished glances of Frau and family, who doubtless thought that they had unwittingly admitted a raving lunatic into their house" (*LM*, 298).

Reviewers of this travel book praised the narrator's "amusing frankness"[42] and even joined in the joking about her husband:

"The book is . . . a lively account of personal adventures and discomforts, which there is some internal evidence to show were shared by Lady Florence's husband."[43] Despite the fact that the narrator of this travel book has "distinguished herself in manly exercises"[44] and disdains ladylike displays of fear, timidity, helplessness, or incompetence, she never openly campaigns for women's rights. And she is even reticent about her flamboyantly original travel costume: "a severely cut serge jacket, a short divided skirt, a broad brimmed felt hat and a pair of bright yellow riding boots."[45] One astounded spectator is reported to have observed: "It is not often that the public have an opportunity of gazing upon a lady dressed in a man's hat and coat, a very short habit and wearing a pair of unmistakeable but untanned Wellingtons. . . . It is said that she can play a decent game of cricket, write a captial newspaper letter, beat most men at billiards, and bivouac as well as any man."[46] In this spectator's mind, clearly, unconventional dress goes hand-in-hand with masculine behavior. But Dixie never discusses her travel apparel or the impression it created; only once does she jokingly allude to the disappointment of Cape Town's inhabitants at not seeing her "poor, travel-stained, well-worn habit of Pretoria renown," which had been dubbed "the looking glass" because it had become so shiny with wear (*LM,* 413). Perhaps her silence on this subject as well as on the topic of women's natural equality was motivated by political considerations. This, after all, is a book designed to influence public opinion about African politics, not about women's rights. To remind the audience too forcefully of the persona's radical views on women would be to jeopardize the cause of Cetshwayo. So Florence Dixie remained mute and allowed her actions to speak for themselves. Her strategy was at least partially successful, for in January 1883 the Zulu king was returned to his throne.

Political Activism, 1882–1905

Dixie's involvement in Cetshwayo's political fortune did not cease with the publication of *In the Land of Misfortune* or with the king's restoration to partial power two months after the book's appearance. The terms under which he was reinstated made his control over his kingdom extremely tenuous: the territory he was granted was only half the size of his original kingdom; it was devoid of the best cattle-grazing land; and it was sandwiched between the realm of chief Zibhebhu, Cetshwayo's arch rival, and a newly created "Zulu Reserve" under British control. Civil war soon broke out, and Cetshwayo was defeated by Zibhebhu. Dixie, who was aware from the beginning that the terms of the reinstatement meant war and defeat for Cetshwayo, wrote angrily to Prime Minister Gladstone, urging him to call together the Zulu chiefs and again restore Cetshwayo to his full power.[47] But her pleas went unheeded. Cetshwayo died, possibly of heart failure, in 1884. His cause remained close to her heart, however; in 1885 she began writing letters on behalf of Cetshwayo's son, Dinzulu, who was being harassed by the Boers. Dixie's relentless Zulu campaign succeeded only in part. Her pen was instrumental in securing Cetshwayo's restoration, but it could not keep him on the throne after his long exile. Her dream of a reunited Zululand and a reunified Zulu nation was never to be fulfilled. Similarly, her arguments for British restraint of the powers of the Boers were to no avail; Boer power in Southern Africa continued to increase until, in 1899, Britain found herself again at war in the land of misfortune.

But partial success, or even absolute defeat, could not deter Florence Dixie from engaging in other political campaigns; indeed, it is as if her labors for Cetshwayo opened a floodgate of political activism which was to channel itself into the Irish Home Rule debate, the suffrage struggle, agitation for animals' rights, and reform of dress, education, diet, and inheritance laws. When Cetshwayo returned to Zululand in 1883, Dixie had already taken up her residence in another land of misfortune—Ireland.

The parallel between the Irish and the Zulus was striking: both were native populations that had been deprived of their birthright by the intervention of Britain. As Dixie wrote in May 1882: "England annexed Ireland, and thereby enriched herself: but what in return did she do, or has she done for this country? . . . she has plundered it. . . ."[48] While Dixie was travelling in South

Africa and arguing Cetshwayo's case, the situation in Ireland was building to a crisis. Severe agricultural depression and escalating evictions of impoverished Irish tenants (there were 10,000 in the year 1880 alone) had produced violent unrest. In 1879 the Land League had been formed to gain Home Rule for Ireland and security for the Irish tenant farmers; in 1880 Charles Stewart Parnell, member of Parliament and campaigner for Home Rule, became its president. In an attempt to deal with Irish problems the Gladstone government proposed a Land Bill which the Land League opposed as insufficiently comprehensive. A rent strike followed and violence flared, culminating in May 1882 with the murder in Phoenix Park, Dublin, of Lord Spencer and Lord Frederick Cavendish, the newly appointed Chief Secretary for Ireland, by a revolutionary group known as the Invincibles.

Dixie, whose mother was a patriotic Irishwoman and who was herself an advocate of Scottish Home Rule, supported legislative independence for Ireland. More than this, she took dramatic personal action to relieve the sufferings of the starving peasants. With the political conscience and the confidence born of her African campaign, Dixie went to western Ireland in the summer of 1882 and began raising money from private and public sources. She collected a total of £6,000, "whereby she was enabled to preserve the rafters over the heads of 20,000 souls."[49] In addition, she began to bombard the newspapers with letters urging Home Rule and criticizing the factionalism of Irish politics: "Away with the Land Leagues, disorder, secret societies, and crime; let Ireland arise and in one body, as of old demand from her sister country her just right. . . ."[50]

Dixie's objection to the Land League, expressed in brief, privately printed pamphlets, like *Ireland and Her Shadow* (1882) and *An Address to the Tenant Farmers and People of Ireland, With Advice and Warning* (1882), were rooted in her strong humanitarianism. The sufferings of individuals outweighed any political victories; the Land League was contemptible because, despite its rhetoric, it had done little to aid the starving peasant. In fact, in a private letter to William Gladsone[51] she accused the Land League of exploiting and exaggerating the sufferings of the Irish worker in order to foment a "terrible revolution." In a letter to the London *Times* (8 March 1883), Dixie reproduced figures she had gleaned from the *Freeman's Journal* (as she had earlier scrutinized the Blue Books for evidence about the Zulu question) which showed that the League had collected £300,000 but only half of that sum was accounted for in its yearly report. She challenged Parnell to explain the discrepancy and to tell why the money had not been put to charitable use; in Parliament, Parnell replied by disputing these calculations and by asserting that the League's money was designed to aid the campaign against landlord oppression. Ironically, the aristocratic Scotswoman who supported Home Rule found herself the bitter enemy of the Protestant Anglo-Irish champion of Home Rule.

Dixie's involvement in Irish politics took a more violent turn than had her activities on behalf of the Zulu. In a letter to Gladstone Dixie begged him to keep secret her private revelations about the Land League, for if they were divulged "my life would not be worth a moment's purchase."[52] Indeed, just two months before writing this, she had been severely shaken by the receipt of a letter bomb. Threatening letters followed and on 17 March 1883, as she was walking her St. Bernard at the back of her home in Windsor, Lady Dixie was jumped by two men dressed as women. The *Times* (19 March 1883) reported: "one of the assailants rushed upon her, knocked her down, and filled her mouth with mud to prevent any cries of assistance being heard. The other then stabbed her with a knife or dagger in two places apparently striking the steel of her stays and preventing the weapon from penetrating the body." As she struggled to wrench the knife from the hands of her attacker, her dog pulled him off, she fainted, and the two men escaped. This "outrage," as the papers called it, perpetrated in the neighborhood of the Queen's residence at Windsor, attracted a great deal of notice and commentary. But the police were unable to uncover any trace of the assailants. For weeks the papers were filled with conflicting pieces of evidence which kept trickling in from the butler, from neighbors, from passersby. As charges of fabrication or exaggeration of the incident arose, Lady Dixie irately refuted them and carefully refrained from directly attributing the attack to Irish partisans (although the evidence and the date did seem to point in that direction). Later she commented that the attack was probably "a matter of intimidation"; but she challenged her foes: "They will not stop me from doing anything I intend to do. They do not know me if they think they can."[53]

Indeed, she was not to be deterred from political activism; soon her energies were channeled into a cause that had concerned her since adolescence, the rights of women. In *Vanity Fair* (16 August 1884) she published "Woman's Mission," an attack on the exclusion of women from the sphere of male labor and male education. Affirming the equality of the sexes and denying that woman's primary mission is motherhood, the article argues for educational parity. Using her own childhood as a paradigm, she urges that women be allowed physical license and encouraged to be "independent and self-supporting." Echoing an important theme of feminist writing of the time,[54] she insists that a woman should receive the same "moral education" as a man and should no longer be "pitchforked into the world without experience" or propelled into motherhood "without the education that should fit her to be one." By cultivating the strength and intelligence of its women, she argues, society is insuring a healthier, more advanced future generation: "I see a mighty race of men and women where once crawled the worms of their former existence."[55]

To actualize this dream, Lady Dixie spent the next twenty years urging the reform of inequitable property, child custody, and inheritance laws. In 1891 she addressed a cheering audience at the inaugural meeting of the Glasgow branch of the Women's Franchise League, a group dedicated to obtaining equal civil and political rights for all women. In a scathing letter to Gladstone, her former ally on the question of Irish Home Rule, she asserted: "No nation is free where its women are degraded by unjust laws."[56] As she had before, Florence Dixie used her pen to wage a war against injustice. In pamphlets and a series of novels, she created a vision of a new, sexually equal world.

The Novels

In the mid-1880s Dixie's days as a hunter and traveller came to an end for medical and financial reasons. Her husband, always an avid gambler on horses, sustained a huge loss in 1883 and was forced to sell the family estate, Bosworth Park, and abandon his extravagant life style. Thus, the couple who had camped out in remote parts of Patagonia settled into a quiet domestic life in various homes. Both Dixies were plagued by ill health in these years: Florence, invalided by rheumatic gout, had to give up the strenuous outdoor life she so loved. These new economic and physical constraints took their psychological toll, as did the suicide of her twin brother in 1891. Her husband notes in his diary that, during this time, she sank for days into "weeping sulks."

But writing seems to have offered Dixie an escape from the sorrows and restrictions of the present. By campaigning for her favorite causes—women's rights, humanitarian treatment of animals, dress reform—she could remain mentally active, even if physically disabled. Writing could take her back in memory to a happier past and could allow her to fabricate a future in which women would be free from discrimination and restraint. Drawing heavily on her own experiences as a child and as a traveller, Lady Dixie wrote a series of novels between 1889 and 1905, whose protagonists are idealized versions of their creator. These strong, confident, athletic women battle against social circumstances and melodramatic villains who reify the evils of those circumstances; they triumph over these enemies through physical daring and moral energy.

Dixie's first novel, *Redeemed in Blood* (1889), encompasses a number of personal experiences: childhood romps in Scotland with her twin, social rebellion in adolescence, travels in Patagonia, and even financial ruin brought about by a husband who gambles. The elaborate plot contains several novels in embryonic form. Volume one begins with the sentimental tale of two first cousins raised as equal companions but barred from marriage by the closeness of their familial relationship. Married to others, they produce children, Maeva and Ronald, who are also reared as soul mates and seem about to relive their parents' fate until the arrival of a dark, handsome, melancholy man, Lord Wrathness. During his stay at the family's castle in Scotland, Wrathness falls in love with the adolescent Maeva Doon, and she not only reciprocates his affection but saves his life by a courageous act. A complication arises in the form of Lady Wrathness, a villainous woman with pencilled eyebrows, who is blackmailing her estranged husband for a murder he did not commit. Volume two takes all the major characters to Patagonia (where they either pursue or flee from each other) and introduces a subplot—the tale of the bankruptcy of Sir Beaufort and Lady Glorie Plunger, who are forced to sell the family estate, Boswell Towers, to meet his gambling debts. As these thinly disguised versions of "Beau" and "Florrie" Dixie wrestle with their economic woes, the events in Patagonia move toward a dramatic climax. Maeva discovers the true murderer and sets about vindicating Lord Wrathness with the help of a young midshipman, Esca Hamilton. Esca, who has fallen in love with Maeva, manages to steal some letters that prove Wrathness's innocence, but the young man is shot by Lady Wrathness, who herself dies soon after out of pique at having her blackmail plot foiled. The example of the heroic Esca, who has redeemed his rival with his own blood, lives on, however, and inspires Maeva and her husband to "raise their fellow-men, to promote justice, alleviate suffering, and hasten on . . . that day when man shall perfect be."[57]

The outlandish plot and flat characters of *Redeemed in Blood* show the limits of Dixie's skill as a novelist. She writes chiefly to reflect upon her own experiences and to promulgate her ideas. Character and incident are subservient to these ends. For instance, she creates a dialogue between Maeva's mother, the unconventional Lady Ettrick, and the Prince of Wales, a house guest of the family. Lady Ettrick lectures the Prince about female education: "If you give them [women] perfect equality in freedom and bringing up, I am much mistaken if women would not take a prominent part in all the great deeds of the world. . . . If the professions were open to them . . . the inducement to marriage would not be so great and the wretched marriages that are yearly born of woman's bondage would never desecrate the earth"

(1:90–91). The physical hardiness and heroic temper of Lady Ettrick's own daughter testify to the wisdom of her ideas on childrearing.

To convince the world that a properly educated woman could "take a prominent part in great deeds," Dixie wrote *Gloriana; or the Revolution of 1900* (1890). An avowedly polemical novel, *Gloriana* uses the form of a dream vision to limn a world in which sexual equality is achieved. Like other feminist novelists of the 1880s and 1890s, Dixie employed an unrealistic literary form to criticize her society and to body forth a new social order which she hoped would become a reality. As Elaine Showalter has observed, in the 1890s women writers began to experiment with short fictional forms: "dreams," "allegories," "fantasias," and "keynotes."[58]

The plot of this visionary work centers on a beautiful feminist, Speranza, and her talented daughter, Gloriana. Having been sold in marriage to a man she despises, Speranza determines to save her daughter from a similar fate. Disguised as a young man, Hector D'Estrange, Gloriana is sent to Eton where she succeeds on every front: she/he is a "splendid boatman, bowler, oarsman, wonderful at racquets, undefeatable in books, beautiful as an Adonis, and clever past expression."[59] In addition, this paragon is an advocate of women's rights who has used his inheritance to establish a school where women can receive educations equal to those of men. Hector's own career proves the ability of women to achieve: elected to Parliament, she/he soon becomes prime minister and changes the suffrage laws. Gloriana is the female messiah whose coming Dixie had anticipated in the 1880s, the "soul far in advance of her generation" who will "strike the chains from the limbs of a womankind fettered by its own ignorance and fear."[60] In a dramatic and cinematic moment, Gloriana rides into the Hall of Liberty mounted on a white charger and surrounded by a regiment of women trained and educated at her school.

Gloriana's male disguise exempts her from sex-based oppression; the other women in the novel are less fortunate. Two of the novel's subplots depict the victimization of women. In one, Florrie Ruglen Desmond, daughter of the Marquis of Douglasdale and a thinly disguised portrait of the author, flees from a man she is being coerced to marry and weds another whom she doesn't love. In the other subplot, Hector's talented mother is abducted by the villainous Lord Westray, whose body is later found buried in Speranza's yard as part of an elaborate plot to discredit Hector/ Gloriana. The prime minister is accused of the murder, tried, and found guilty, but is rescued by the regiment of women commanded by the valiant Florrie Desmond. After these dramatic incidents, the plot becomes increasingly improbable. Hector, who in the course of the murder trial has been unmasked as a woman, flees to the country with her best friend-lover, is betrayed by a traitorous female follower (who later repents and takes an assassin's bullet meant for Gloriana), and seemingly drowns in an accident. But, in a far-fetched conclusion, Gloriana returns unharmed, the new male prime minister resigns his office to her, and an era of unexampled reform and prosperity commences. The novel ends with the vision of a world radically remade along the lines of Dixie's imagination: absolute personal freedom is accompanied by political independence for Ireland, Wales, and Scotland, who willingly join Britain in a federated empire. As in the earlier *Isola,* Dixie demonstrates in *Gloriana* that the extirpation of sexual inequality leads to an Utopian world. For Dixie, the female author is the pioneer of social reform; she would have concurred with the feminist Mrs. Haweis that "in women writers' hands lies the regeneration of the world," and that they write with "tongues of fire—cleansing, repairing, beautifying the page of the world's history."[61]

To prepare new generations for this reconstituted world, Dixie began writing children's books that challenged sexual stereotypes and presented models of powerful, active, independent women. Using her knowledge of South America and some of her own experiences, Dixie wrote *The Two Castaways; or Adventures in Patagonia* (1889) and *Aniwee; or the Warrior Queen: A Tale of the Araucanian Indians* (1890). In both of these books the fearless adolescent twins, Harry and Topsie Vane, wage war, battle ferocious animals, and escape unscathed and unchastened from situations of extreme peril. Having been shipwrecked in Patagonia on the way to meet their father, an admiral stationed in the south Atlantic, the Vanes soon fall in with a band of Tehuecle Indians. From the beginning the narrator makes her polemical purpose clear by exhorting male readers always to treat females fairly and by reminding them that, if their sisters seem "weak and feeble," it is only because of their "training and education."[62] None of the women in this tale, however, betray any weaknesses. As physically hardy as her brother, Topsie is a better shot than he with a rifle and repeatedly displays more maturity and common sense. Among the Indians whom the Vanes befriend is another remarkable female, Aniwee, the rebellious fourteen-year-old daughter of the tribe's chief. As the narrator observes, Aniwee "felt the bondage of her sex, and, like many of her white sisters, desired to change it into freedom" (128). Disgusted by the domestic slavery of the Indian woman, Aniwee determines to be a warrior and to prove that "a girl can be as brave, aye, braver than a boy" (136). Her heroism earns Aniwee the right to be a warrior and ride out in battle against the Indians' enemy, the "Cristianos" (as the white Christian residents of Argentina are called).

Once Aniwee has joined the warrior ranks, the plot becomes that of a classic children's adventure tale, with danger that is never creditably threatening, legendary and fantastic creatures, and fierce battles in which the forces of good always win. The conventionality of the narrative frame contrasts with the unconventional perspective of the story, however. Not only is this a feminist tale with female heroes, it is also a narrative in which Indians are the "good guys." The champion of other native peoples, Dixie here portrays the Indians as a brave race with an interesting, complex culture, a people who have been exploited and mistreated by white men. In these children's books Dixie expresses a sympathy for and understanding of the Indians which far surpasses that found in her travel narrative, *Across Patagonia.*

Like most romances, *The Two Castaways* ends with a marriage and a reunion: Aniwee is betrothed to the son of the chief of the Araucanian tribe and the shipwrecked children are restored to their father, who has come to Patagonia to search for them. In the sequel, *Aniwee; or the Warrior Queen,* the same cast of characters is assembled in Patagonia after a three-year separation. Although the twins have changed little in that time, Aniwee has married, borne a daughter, been widowed through treachery, and is now the first Queen Regent of the tribe. The shy but brave fourteen-year-old girl of the earlier book is now an absolute monarch, whose word is "law" and whose army is "efficient and devoted."[63] One strand of the novel's plot deals with the attempts by traitorous Indians to undermine that devotion, unseat Aniwee, and kidnap her daughter, the heir to the throne. The other plot strand comprises the kidnapping of Topsie by a hirsute aboriginal people called "Traucos" and the attempts to rescue her. The rescue party not only traverses some of the wildest and most beautiful scenery in Patagonia, it also discovers Aniwee's husband, who is not dead but a prisoner of the Traucos. After finding a legendary gold mine, reminiscent of that in H. Rider Haggard's *King Solomon's Mines,* and surviving an earthquake, the whole party returns to camp to fight a bloody battle against the Christians. Again, the novel concludes with the reuniting of separated families; this time, however, the conclusion also anticipates a peaceful future because the dispute between the Indians and the whites is being mediated by the twins' aunt and uncle.

Both of these books reveal Dixie's shortcomings as a novelist: melodramatic plots, static characters, an absolutism of good and evil, and a penchant for preaching. For instance, at a moment of high tension in the narrative, when Topsie has volunteered to scale a dangerously steep cliff in order to save her compatriots trapped in a collapsing mine, the narrator interrupts: "Yet in the face of this courageous proposal, this high resolve so modestly and quietly put, there are many who still presume to train the boy up to believe himself the girl's superior in daring, skill, strength, and physical activity" (*Aniwee,* 237).

On the other hand, these tales do display vivid descriptions of the Patagonian landscape, brisk narrative of physical activities, especially hunts, and passionate anger at inhumanity and injustice to women, to animals, or to Indians. The woman who had not responded intensely to the Indians' plight when she visited Patagonia, espoused it ten years later in these two children's books and also in an article published in the *Westminster Review*.[64] In that piece she claimed that contact with white men, as well as the drunkenness that resulted from that interaction, was ruining the Indians, and she advocated the establishment of a British trading company in Patagonia as a way of preventing any future degradation of Indian culture.

But it was not the future so much as the past that occupied Dixie in the final years of the nineteenth century and the early years of the twentieth. The writing of children's books plunged Florence Dixie into reflections on her own childhood, particularly on those forces that had thwarted her development and shaped her personality. Increasingly, she realized that conventional religion was the root cause of sexual and social injustice. Challenging the premises of traditional religion in an article first published in *The Agnostic Annual*, she ridiculed traditional notions about God and attacked "the charter of woman's serfdom, and, as a consequence of man's degradation. It, like all superstitious God-books, is the outcome of ignorance ruled by selfishness."[65]

The final works of her life were accounts of her own struggles from childhood onwards with the narrow social and moral codes of her times. *The Story of Ijain, or The Evolution of a Mind* (1903) exposes the harmful effects of orthodox religious training on sensitive children and espouses a Wordsworthian "natural piety" as the ideal religion. Ijain, a name by which Dixie herself was known, is another autobiographical heroine who, like her creator, rebels against the "unnatural" and unjust laws of her society. In a series of episodes loosely strung together, the novel traces Ijain from her childhood freedom among the hills of Scotland with her large, congenial family, to her incarceration in a number of schools where she feels harassed and misunderstood, to her travels through Europe and her meeting with the handsome midshipman, Esca. The novel concludes as Ijain, who has wandered the nocturnal London streets and observed the economic and social oppression of her society, poises on the threshold of a new life dedicated to the good of humankind. The novel's message, according to W.

Stewart Ross, Dixie's friend and the editor of the *Agnostic Journal,* is "Help Man, and, if it so please you, call it worshipping God."[66]

Ijain's preface advertised it as the first part of a major opus, twenty-five years in the making. The second installment of this autobiography, *Izra, or a Child of Solitude,* appeared in the *Agnostic Journal* from 1903 to 1905, when Dixie's sudden death from diphtheria brought it to an end. In this work the protagonist has been split into two characters: a female, Isa Delamore, who is a fictionalized Florence Dixie, and a male, Izra, who is a fantasy self. Izra, a contemporary Galahad, wanders the globe doing good and philosophizing about the state of human civilization; Isa, his twin sister, is a wife, a mother of two sons, and a political activist who espouses the cause of Cetshwayo, women, etc. The loosely structured, episodic narrative encompasses travel writing, utopian fantasy, and polemic on topics like cruelty to animals, the oppression of women, and contemporary politics. One commentator on the work observed that it "defies classification": "It is not a novel, it is not a book of travels."[67]

Through the character of Izra, Dixie voices her dreams of the world as it might be; through Isa she rehearses her criticism of the world as it is. Isa even writes articles, which are quoted extensively in the text, that Dixie herself penned in the 1880s. More than any earlier work, however, *Izra* promulgates Dixie's increasingly radical ideas about sexuality. Through the persona of a Tibetan monk, she advocates a "sex science": serious study of the nature of sexual attraction; open, natural sex education for children; and population control based on scientific knowledge. Anticipating the arguments of modern feminism, she predicts that future women will have control over their own biological processes: "The free woman will own her own children and never consent to submit to enforced motherhood. Reproduction and sexual intercourse will cease to be regarded as impossible of separation."[68]

Florence Dixie's sudden death on 7 November 1905 prevented her from witnessing the fulfillment of any of her dreams for women or for the human race. Her obituary in the London *Times* noted condescendingly: "Though ardently convinced of the truth and righteousness of her somewhat peculiar views, Lady Florence Dixie had an attractive and attaching personality" (8 November 1905). Less kind but still superior in tone are contemporary writers' assertions that she was "a scatterbrained enthusiast" or an "erratic," emotionally unstable woman.[69] On the other hand, those who shared her "peculiar views" hailed Dixie as a courageous social reformer, and "as brave a human being as ever lived."[70] Perhaps her mother best captured Florence Dixie's character: "Florence says that the only way to carry a citadel is to undermine it and then dash at it. No use sitting down and looking at it."[71] Consistently and determinedly, Florence Dixie attacked the citadels of social injustice, imperialism, and sexual prejudice in her world. In travel writings, political pamphlets, poems, and novels, she not only undermined these structures but dared to imagine a world reconstituted. Herself a traveller to new physical worlds, she took her readers on a mental odyssey to a new earth, harmonious, just, Edenic.

Chapter Four
Mary Henrietta Kingsley
Family and Childhood

"The whole of my childhood and youth was spent at home, in the house and garden," confessed Mary Kingsley, the African traveller, in the year before her death. "The living outside world I saw little of and cared less for . . . I knew nothing of play and such things. . . . I had a great amusing world of my own other people did not know, or care about—that was the books in my father's library."[1] This lonely, shy child, who devoured books like Burton's *Anatomy of Melancholy*, Johnson's *Robberies and Murders of the Most Notorious Pirates*, and Bayle's *Dictionary*, was to become in her thirties a celebrated traveller, a best-selling author, a popular lecturer, and an influential figure in African colonial politics. This daughter of eccentric parents, forced into a premature responsibility by her home life and isolated from her peers, was to emerge as not only one of the most famous but one of the most literate and personally complex of nineteenth-century female travellers.

Mary Henrietta Kingsley, the first child of George Kingsley and Mary Bailey, was born in Islington on 13 October 1862, four days after her parents' marriage.[2] Within a year of her birth the family moved to Highgate, where they lived for sixteen years. Here a son, Charles George, was born in 1864. Mary's father, an "attractive, lithe . . . man, alert with the warm passionate spirit of life,"[3] was himself the son of a family of eminent Victorians known for their literary talent, adventurousness, love of natural beauty, and their tendency to exhaust themselves in "rapidly successive outbreaks of intellectual brilliancy" (*Notes*, 1). The four children of the Reverend Charles Kingsley who survived to adulthood—Charles, George, Henry, and Charlotte—all were authors: in the second generation, Charles's daughter Mary became the novelist "Lucas Malet" while George's Mary wrote three books—*Travels in West Africa* (1897), *West African Studies (1899)*, and *The Story of West Africa* (1899)—and edited her father's writings in a volume entitled *Notes on Sport and Travel* (1900). Prefacing this selection of articles and letters is a memoir of her father by Mary H. Kingsley, a piece which provides a detailed picture of her childhood and that of her father's family as well.

Undoubtedly the most famous member of that family was Charles Kingsley—clergyman, poet, novelist, the "muscular Christian" who advocated athletic "manliness" as the attribute of a Christian gentleman. A Christian Socialist influenced by F. D. Maurice, Charles Kingsley reminded the church of its social responsibility and limned the sufferings of the poor in novels like *Yeast* (1848), *Alton Locke* (1850),and the children's classic, *The Water Babies* (1863). A man of nervous, restless temperament, Charles Kingsley wrote historical novels and articles on natural history, while also serving as professor of English at the newly formed Queens College, London, and professor of Modern History at Cambridge University before dying at fifty-four from lung congestion.

Henry Kingsley exorcised his restless spirit through travel and writing: at age twenty-three he left Oxford for the gold fields of Australia, where he drifted through the jobs of miner, stock rider, and mounted policeman. Returning to England after a five-year absence, he wrote several novels, including his most famous, *Ravenshoe* (1862). For eighteen months he edited the *Edinburgh Daily Review*. According to his niece, Henry Kingsley "squandered alike brilliant talents and brilliant opportunities without attaining happiness" *(Notes,* 6). When he died of cancer at age forty-six, Henry left behind an impoverished widow who, in later years, received financial help from George's daughter Mary.[4]

Although publicly she attested to the undiminished affection of the Kingsleys for each other, privately, Mary Kingsley revealed that her father had "cut himself away from" his brothers.[5] The reasons for the rift are unclear; perhaps it was caused by George's agnosticism or perhaps by the family's disapproval of his marriage to a woman of rather obscure origin, who may have been his cook or landlady[6] and who was pregnant with his child. Mary Kingsley never admitted to her own narrow escape from illegitimacy, nor did she ever discuss the Kingsley family's reaction to her father's conduct, but she did tell her publisher, George Macmillan, that she "detested" the "humbug and equivocation" of her uncles.[7] Although she disparaged her immediate relations, Mary Kingsley frequently romanticized her remote ancestors, giving them credit for the "blood" which made her achievements possible: "I come of a generation of Danes who . . . [found] light enough to fight by with their Morning Stars; and who, later on, were soldiers in the Low Countries and slave owners in the West Indies."[8] Unabashedly proud of these forebears who were not "humbugs," Kingsley saw her father as the embodiment both of their adventurous spirit and the code of honor of a "noble, perfect Englishman."

Trained as a doctor, George Kingsley used his profession as a means of indulging his passions—travel, hunting, and literature. In 1850 he became the private physician to the first Marquis of Aylesbury; subsequently he occupied the same post with five other noblemen. Not only did he thus gain access to these wealthy men's libraries and to their rich game parks where, in his own words, he "slaughter[ed] salmon, stags, and fowl at a most fearful rate . . . from six in the morning to nine at night" (*Notes*, 26), he also travelled with them through the Mediterranean, Egypt, the western United States, Japan, and the South Seas. To his wife and children at home, he sent letters brimming with adventures—shipwrecks, encounters with grizzly bears, tales of cannibalism—written with a vivid descriptive power, an informal, slangy diction, and a comic sense that foreshadow his daughter's style in her travel narratives. For the public he produced several books and articles, including *South Sea Bubbles; by the Earl and the Doctor* (1872) written with the Earl of Pembroke, but his daughter estimated that he had enough material "to fill volumes" (*Notes*, 192). His admiring child once compared her father to the celebrated Richard Burton in possessing an "enthusiasm for scholarship, coupled with . . . [a] power of action" (*Notes*, 191).

The peripatetic George's sojourns at home appear to have been stormy because of his "volcanic" temper, which often collided with the will of his adoring but independent daughter. She later recalled having to "dodge" a copy of Brand's *Dictionary of the Arts and Sciences* "temporarily diverted into use as a projectile in consequence of some conduct of mine"; she knew, however, that "all would be well, provided I went away and was quiet for a time. No one in his family knew half so much of his temper as I did" (*Notes*, 195). These outbursts were triggered by her noisy pet fighting cocks, by her attempts to tidy her father's study, and by her swearing. Once, an exasperated Dr. Kingsley seized his daughter and "carried her horizontally downstairs," demanding: "Where does this child get its language from?" (*Notes*, 196).

If life with father involved dodging books and catering to the tastes of a man whom his friend F. H. H. Guillemard described as "a queer fish in many ways,"[9] existence during his long absences was a strain on the physical and emotional resources of the family. Mrs. Kingsley, a "benevolent woman" and a skilled business manager who shielded her husband from the "petty cares" of life, appears to have literally shut herself up in the house and seen no one when he was away. Her daughter noted that "for months at a time she was kept in an unbroken strain of nervous anxiety about him . . . one long nervous strain which robbed her of all pleasure in life outside the sphere of her home duty and the companionship of books" (*Notes*, 204). For months on end she had no idea of her husband's whereabouts; moreover, when his letters did arrive they cavalierly alluded to brushes with death. Soon after his daughter's birth George Kingsley wrote from the Mediterranean: "You must be surprised to see where I have got to, I had an offer of a cruise . . . and so came round here. Lucky for us that we are here, for we were very nearly lost on the night we sailed" (*Notes*, 31).

Mrs. Kingsley's psychological tension seems to have been complicated by financial strains during her husband's absences. When Mary was an infant, Henry Kingsley was forced to write to his publishers, the Macmillan firm, for an advance so that he could send money to his brother's family: "When he is abroad, I have to keep both houses," Henry complained, launching into an account of George's failure to provide the funds necessary to care for his wife and child (January 1864). Although generally reluctant to fault her father, Mary Kingsley did once criticize his treatment of his family: "I used to contemplate with a feeling of irritation the way in which my father used to reconcile . . . it to himself, that because he had a wife and family it was his dire and awful duty to go and hunt grizzly bears in a Red Indian infested district" (*Notes,* 202). The ironic humor here cannot quite camouflage the resentment felt by a neglected child. The adult reflects apologetically: "I fancy now that I was wrong to have felt any irritation with him." Even after Dr. Kingsley abandoned his travels in 1879 and the family moved to Bexley, Kent, for the sake of his wife's health, Mrs. Kingsley seems to have remained a reclusive figure whom friends seldom saw and whom at least one visitor considered "not quite *compos mentis.*"[10]

Her family situation thrust upon the young Mary Kingsley's shoulders a heavy burden of adult responsibility. Not only was she her "mother's chief officer from the day I could carry a duster" but she was also the chief "handyman" of the delapidating house in Kent. At an age when other Victorian girls were learning to embroider, to flirt, to sing, and to play the piano, she was teaching herself how to repair burst pipes, with the aid of "that delightful paper *The English Mechanic,*" or was experimenting with the production of land mines from a tin of gunpowder and a tub of liquid manure in the backyard—with disastrous consequences for the family washing! For this "thin pale girl of middle height, with straight fair hair and blue eyes,"[11] books and *The English Mechanic* were her primary companions. Her younger brother, who figures little in her accounts of her childhood and adolescence, seems to have offered neither companionship nor help. When Mary does refer to him, it is as one of her patients whose "delicate health" she must guard. Throughout her life Kingsley devoted herself to Charles's welfare, keeping house for him when he was in England and fretting over his illness:

"Master Charles has driven me distraught with a dreadful cough and pain in his lung. Of course he would not see a doctor or allow the subject to be mentioned."[12] This childhood training in loneliness, self-denial, and self-reliance produced a woman who was capable of enduring long periods of isolation in the African bush and of using her wits to extricate herself from perilous situations.

It was only because of ingenuity and determination that Mary Kingsley was able to gain an education. Although later in life she spoke humorously of her struggle to instruct herself, clearly this woman was always angry and frustrated about her haphazard education. For instance, having developed a "passionate devotion" to chemistry, she turned to her father's collection of alchemical literature and obsolete chemical texts for instructions:

After most carefully getting up all the information these could give me, I happened on a gentleman who knew modern chemistry. . . . He said he had not heard anything so ridiculous for years, and recommended that I should be placed in a museum as a compendium of exploded chemical theories, which hurt my feelings very much, and I cried bitterly at not being taught such things. My home authorities said I had not business to want to be taught such things. (*M.A.P.*, 469)

But the woman whose scientific curiosity would later lead her to study fetishes and cannibalism, as well as navigation of canoes and steamers, wanted to know all "such things." Given a copy of Craik's *Pursuit of Knowledge Under Difficulties,* she determined to stop "whining about looking for someone to teach me" and to emulate those who "had invented the steam engine from observing the habits of tea kettles." Using libraries and her brother's books, she persevered, and, when the family moved to Cambridge in 1883 so that Charles could study at the university, his sister "continued her mathematics, studied Darwin, Huxley, Lubbock, Tylor, and the great principles of modern science."[13]

Her haphazard, self-conducted education reinforced Kingsley's sense of insecurity and ignited an anger which smoldered for many years. After she had written two successful books, she wrote to Macmillan (January 1899): "I don't know if I ever revealed to you the fact that being allowed to learn German was all the paid-for education I ever had—2000 pounds was spent on my brother, I still hope not in vain." The resentment that vibrates in that final phrase was, in fact, well-founded, since Charles never finished any scholarly projects and spent his adulthood as a dilettantish traveller in the Orient; while his uneducated sister published and lectured voluminously but worried about her ability to write, to construct theories based on observations, and to speak without dropping her "h's." Ironically, after her death Charles planned a biography of his talented sister which he never completed and the materials for which he destroyed.

Mary Kingsley's German lessons were allowed so that she could become an "underworker" on her father's scholarly projects. George Kingsley, who had been in youth an avid naturalist, had translated some German fiction and planned several literary works; he seemed to his daughter "a treasure house of learning profound and varied" (*Notes*, 191). When he retired from his travels in 1879, her father devoted himself to "all manner of branches of obscure learning, mainly . . . early English literature and Semitic tradition" (*Notes*, 192). During her adolescence Mary Kingsley was allowed to do "odd jobs," collecting travellers' accounts and reading German authors for her father's projected work on the ideas behind primitive sacrificial rites. Such early training in the rudiments of ethnography and the techniques of field research later proved invaluable to her own study of African culture. Undoubtedly, it also stimulated her longing to travel to distant lands.

But even scholarly research had to be subordinated to domestic obligations, which after 1888 included nursing both an ailing mother and a father with rheumatic fever. These years of "work and watching and anxiety" and of a depressingly narrow life (*M.A.P.*, 269) were suddenly terminated in 1892 when both parents died within six weeks. These painful, demanding years deepened Mary Kingsley's sense of duty to her fellow human beings, a devotion which manifested itself in her compassionate nursing of Africans in the bush, of white traders suffering from malaria or delirium tremens, and of Boer prisoners-of-war lan-

guishing in filthy, understaffed hospitals. Her early life strength-
ened Kingsley's often-repeated conviction that she was valued by
other people only so long as she could serve them. Thus, in later
years, she kept house for, nursed, and made excuses for her brother
Charles; she even arranged her travels to suit his needs. She felt
it was her duty to serve him "as long as he wants me to do so."[14]
A friend identified the essence of Kingsley's personality: "Every
personal hope and fear had been laid aside, and nothing left but
service to all who needed it."[15] The corollary of this self-abne-
gating sense of duty, however, was a "dark and solitary self"[16]
which can be discerned in her private letters and can occasionally
be glimpsed behind the public mask she adopts. She confessed
to a friend: "I am really a very melancholy person inside. But I
don't show that part of myself. I feel that I have no right to
anyone's sympathy."[17] Feeling herself to be an outsider permanently exiled from the company of "normal" people, Kingsley
identified her home as "the valley of the shadow of death."

Those years of service to others, then, seem to have fostered
a radical sense of insignificance bordering on anonymity: "I am
no more a human being than a gust of wind is. I have never had
a human individual life. I have always been the doer of odd-
jobs—and I lived in the joys, sorrows, and worries of other
people."[18] Perhaps it was the belief that she had no individual
life that led Kingsley to embrace causes with such ferocious enthusiasm. By becoming the spokeswoman for the African, for the
white trader, or for a political cause, she could gain an identity,
a sense of personal value, that was otherwise unavailable to her.

Because the notes, journals, and correspondence in her brother's
possession were destroyed after her death, it is difficult to construct a complete emotional profile of Kingsley's first thirty years,
or to account adequately for her daring decision to venture alone
to West Africa in August 1893, or to explain some of her seemingly paradoxical views. Only by reading between the lines of
her surprisingly confessional public statements in later life; by
scrutinizing her remaining letters in private collections, particularly those to her friends Major Matthew Nathan, John Holt,
Alice S. Green, and Stephen Gwynn; by weighing the discoveries

of her first biographer, Stephen Gwynn, as well as those of later biographers like Olwen Campbell and Cecil Howard; and finally by analyzing the conflicting voices heard in her self-presentation, can contemporary readers begin to comprehend the intricate character of this woman traveller.

Despite its loneliness and emotional stress, Kingsley's childhood seems to have been an appropriate apprenticeship to a life of independence and unconventional travel. Freed by her father's absences and her mother's invalidism from parental dominance, allowed to engage in "masculine" activities and to develop her interest in science, she was uniquely prepared for travel in places where "feminine" squeamishness in the face of violence, immorality, or primitive living conditions would have been not only absurd but dangerous. That Kingsley chose to travel through Africa with only a few bearers and to live "like a native" is consistent with her view of herself as a woman "roustabout"— tough, able to cope with whatever man or nature might cast her way. She scorned prissy lady travellers like May French Sheldon who brought with them all the comforts of home and insisted that African chiefs wear trousers in their presence. Sometimes Mary Kingsley even spoke of herself as a male traveller, a "practical seaman," or a "trading man."

On the other hand, Kingsley thought of herself as a lady and longed to be considered feminine. She seems to have felt deeply her early exclusion from the female world of courting, emotional intrigue, fashion, and love. In her travels she took care to appear in "lady-like" apparel, even after a three-day trek through leech-ridden swamps. Although she lavished praise on beautiful African women, Kingsley herself dressed in a consciously old-fashioned, "almost farcical" way[19] which she staunchly defended as of practical value in the bush. Spurning the trousers adopted by more radical women travellers, she donned a long, black woolen skirt, high-necked blouse, and small black hat which, in the opinion of a friend, made her look "less like an explorer than anyone I ever saw."[20] Repeatedly she reminds her readers of her femininity, often in a jesting tone of voice: "I am a most lady-like old person and yet get constantly called 'Sir.' . . . I never even wear a masculine collar and tie, and as for encasing the more earthward extremities of my anatomy in—you know what I mean—well, I would rather perish on the public scaffold."[21] With tongue in cheek, she describes a trader who, mistaking her for a man because of the pronomial ambiguity of African languages, addressed her as "My Dear Old Man" and offered a pair of dry trousers to the exhausted traveller. Mary comments on this misunderstanding: "Had there been any smelling salts . . . in this subdivision of the Ethiopian region I should have forthwith fainted on reading this, but I well knew there was not, so I blushed until the steam from my soaking clothes . . .went up in a cloud. . . ." (*TWA*, 502). Interestingly, this passage, intended to affirm her femininity, also points to the absurdity of stereotypical female behavior like fainting and blushing. Common sense and practicality dominate even a lady's conduct in Africa.

The tone of self-mockery here and in much of her writing derives from this same central ambivalence about her own identity. Feeling herself to be slightly ludicrous in the eyes of others, she often exploited this perception to create high comedy in her narratives. Moreover, she seems to have cultivated her own absurdity to create the public persona of an eccentric old lady. The Liverpool and Manchester traders called her "Our Aunt" and the inhabitants of the West Coast "Only Me" because of her habit of appearing unexpectedly at a remote station in the bush with one cheery announcement that "it's only me." Perhaps this persona and her incongruous dress amused her, perhaps they served as masks for a feeling, vulnerable self. She once confessed to Stephen Gwynn that she had "plenty of " feelings but hid them "from the eyes of almost everyone I know . . . they are savage things that would make people, who have not got that sort of feeling inside them, shrink from me. There! That is the reason why I am 'elusive.' I know it and it is malice aforethought."[22] This woman—so adventurous, so fearless, so talented, yet so convinced of her own insignificance and inadequacy—chose to travel to a part of the world whose political and social complexity equalled her own.

The Lure of West Africa

If you were to ask the average Englishman of Mary Kingsley's day about West Africa, he would probably tell you—as Kingsley's friends told her—that it was "the deadliest spot on earth" (*TWA,* 2). If he were an armchair geographer he might remember that several famous British explorers had ventured there: Mungo Park to the upper reaches of the Niger in 1797 and 1805; David Livingstone in his famous trans-Africa journey of 1853–56 through Angola to the coastal town of Luanda; Richard Burton, while a consul in the Bights of Benin and Biafra, to Lagos, Dahomey, and the peaks of the Cameroon Mountains. He would undoubtedly know that, from the 1820s onward, the area had been known as the "white man's grave" because of the high mortality rate of the ex-slaves from Britain who had settled in Sierra Leone and of the men who had joined the government-sponsored Niger Expedition in 1841. Certainly he would tell you tales about cannibalism, witch doctors, human sacrifice, and polygamy.

However, if you questioned a member of one of the great trading firms of Liverpool or Manchester, or alternatively a member of a mission society, you would receive a more detailed, politically biased report. For, throughout the nineteenth century, it was the traders and missionaries who urged a reluctant Britain toward commitments in West Africa. The traders sought markets for British manufactured goods among the populace and access to the rubber and palm oil available in the interior sections of what is now Nigeria. The missionaries and philanthropists tried to halt the slave trade, to Christianize and thereby (they believed) civilize the African. As the trading firms sent agents to remote places in the bush to establish "factories" or trading stations, so the various missionary societies dispatched their members to found churches and schools. Although hostile to each other, each of these groups wanted the British government to guarantee a certain level of protection to its members. But until the 1880s the government resisted all pleas for increased involvement in West Africa: "London was dead against extending territorial responsibilities and warned its local agents to keep to coastal and riverine influence. . . . With its lethal climate, its barbaric tribes, its disorders and difficult communications, . . . its lack of disciplined labour and purchasing power, West Africa seemed no place for colonial expansion."[23] In fact, in 1863 a select Committee of the House of Commons recommended a policy of British withdrawal from all West Coast possessions except Sierra Leone.

However, this indifference to West Africa yielded, in the 1880s, to an active interest in amassing territory around the Congo and Niger Rivers. During the 1880s and 1890s European powers were locked in a "scramble" for territory in West Africa and for access to West African trade. In the eighties the French seized Dahomey, thus driving a wedge between the Gold Coast and Lagos, both under British control; in addition, the French began to make inroads on the Upper Niger. In 1885 a conference in Berlin divided the Congo basin among European powers and split the Niger between France, which got control of the upper reaches of the river, and England, which was allowed hegemony on the lower part of the river. In addition, a third political force emerged in this area in the mid-1880s. George Goldie, director of a large British trading firm, had been making a series of treaties with local chiefs which gave him a trade monopoly over a large parcel of land in present-day Nigeria. When he received a charter in 1886 to establish the Royal Niger Company, Goldie, much to the chagrin of the French and his British trade rivals in the Oil River ports on the Niger delta, assumed quasi-governmental powers by levying taxes, restricting trade, and policing his company's large holdings.

The international and intranational rivalries accelerated in the early 1890s. Britain and France sent competing exploratory parties into the interior of West Africa to make trade treaties. Armed British and French groups confronted each other in towns to which each laid claim. In a politically tense environment, a boundary commission was constituted in 1892 to establish peacefully the border between French Senegal and British Sierra Leone. In these same years Africans were beginning to chafe under the trade restrictions imposed upon them in their own lands by the Royal Niger Company. The resentment of the inhabitants of the island of Brass finally exploded in an armed rebellion against Goldie's government in 1895.

This, then, was the volatile political milieu into which Kingsley the novice traveller ventured alone in 1893. She chose West Africa for several personal and scientific reasons which she advanced with varying degrees of seriousness depending on her audience. On her maiden voyage to the Canaries, she had encountered several "Old Coasters" returning from West Africa. These tough, salty characters and their grisly tales clearly fascinated her. Perhaps, in their voices she heard echoes of her father's descriptions of his adventures. Certainly the perilous country they described offered Kingsley a personal testing ground in which she could compete with her father—and even best him—by visiting a land he had never seen. Hence, the elation evident in the opening paragraph of *Travels in West Africa* in which Mary Kingsley describes herself as possessing for the first time in her life "five or six months which were not heavily forestalled" and "feeling like a boy with a new half-crown." Kingsley goes on to explain that she decided on West Africa because: " 'Go and learn your tropics,' said Science. Where on earth am I to go, I wondered . . ". so I got down an atlas and saw that either South America or West Africa must be my destination" (*TWA*, 1). The humorous tone and the mock dialogue with "Science" suggest a casual and unscholarly intent. Yet, later in life, she offered a more professional explanation of her journey: "When there were no more odd jobs . . . to do at home, I, out of my life in books, found something for which I had been taught German . . . the study of early religion and law, and for it I had to go to West Africa, and I went there" (*M.A.P.*, 469). In a lecture during the last year of her life she adopted the persona of the dutiful daughter of the dedicated scientist: "My motive for going to West Africa was study . . . to complete a great book my father . . . had left at his death unfinished. . . . [He] knew the natives of the South Sea Islands and the Red Indians of North America personally. . . . What the Africans thought about religion and law he could not so easily find out" (*WAS*, xxii).

By convincing herself that she was going to Africa because of duty, "the religion I was brought up in,"[24] Kingsley could follow in her father's footsteps while also competing with him. Her eagerness to amass scientific justifications for her trip led her to visit Dr. A. Günther of the British Museum to discover what zoological specimens she could most profitably collect. They decided on fish, and Kingsley gathered such an impressive sample on her first trip that the museum gave her an official collector's kit for her subsequent journey. As a woman, she may have felt a particular need to establish her credentials as a serious traveller, not an idle wanderer; just two years before Kingsley's first journey, the *Spectator,* in an article sneeringly entitled "The Lady-Errant," had dismissed Mrs. Sheldon's travels because they had "no scientific end" but were motivated by "merely feminine curiosity."[25]

In a letter to Major Matthew Nathan (12 March 1899), Kingsley confesses a far darker, private motive for going to Africa: "Dead tired and feeling no one had need of me any more, when my Mother and Father died within six weeks of each other in '92, . . . I went down to West Africa to die. West Africa amused me and was kind to me and was scientifically interesting—and did not want to kill me just then." Although Stephen Gwynn takes this as proof of a latent suicidal urge, later biographers have pointed out that this letter, written seven years after the fact, expresses Kingsley's exhaustion and depression in 1899, not her mood in 1892.[26] Moreover, this statement must be juxtaposed both to Kingsley's precautions against contracting fever in West Africa and her remark in a lecture during the last year of her life that "It was no desire to get killed and eaten that made me go and associate with the tribes with the worst reputation for cannibalism and human sacrifice; but just because such tribes were the best for me to study. . . ."[27]

Undoubtedly, Mary Kingsley had a deep streak of melancholy in her personality and a conviction of her personal worthlessness; moreover, she felt particularly lost when the domestic and familial obligations, which had constrained her life for so many years, suddenly disappeared. And, when she was in Africa, although she took careful measures to avoid the dread fever, she also delighted in putting herself into perilous situations in defiance of the advice of friends. To survive the danger and then to laugh at their concerns amused her. For example, after completing her dangerous journey through the territory between the Ogowé and the Rembwé Rivers, Kingsley reported that Mr. Hudson, a trader, "persisted in his opinion that my intentions and ambitions were suicidal," and concluded that he "took me down the Woermann Road, the ensuing Sunday, as it were on a string" (*TWA*, 352). Perhaps Kingsley did go to West Africa in a despairing mood and did court danger in order to prove herself and achieve the status of survivor. But ironically through her experiences in the "white man's grave" Kingsley found reason for living.

The First Trip

When the solitary, primly attired Miss Kingsley, who carried herself "with a curious stiffness,"[28] boarded the unkempt cargo boat *Lagos* in August 1893, the other passengers thought she was a spy from "the World's Women's Temperance Association . . . collecting shocking details . . . on the liquor traffic" (*TWA*, 5). But neither a teetotaler nor a prude, Mary Kingsley plunged herself into the rowdy life on this steamer bound for West Africa, collecting details, not about the liquor traffic, but about practical seamanship, the "natural history" of mariners, the cultures of coastal Africans, and survival tactics for life in the bush. The instructions offered by her friend, the ship's Captain Murray, and by government officials and traders on board proved invaluable—Kingsley credited her shipboard education with saving her life "countless times" in Africa. Her fellow passengers were likely to be prolix, however, on two topics: death and disease. With a dramatic flair and a Dickensian eye for absurdity and the macabre, Kingsley records a typical dinner conversation:

One of the Agents would look at the Captain . . . and say, "You remember J., Captain?" "Knew him well," says the Captain; "why I brought him out his last time, poor chap!" then follows full details of the pegging-out of J., and his funeral &c. Then a Government official who had been out before, would kindly turn to a colleague out for the first time, and say, "Brought any dress clothes with you?" The unfortunate new-comer, scenting an allusion to a more cheerful phase of Coast life, gladly answers in the affirmative. "That's right," says the interlocutor; "You want them to wear to funerals." (*WAS,* 6)

Even such a gruesome discussion, though, could not make repulsive the land she described as "La Belle Dame Sans Merci," the land of irresistible "charm," which also offered the traveller "any amount of work . . . worth doing" (*TWA,* 11).

Kingsley left no connected narrative of this initial voyage, but her path through Africa can be reconstructed from scattered allusions in her published writings. The *Lagos* made its way past the Canary Islands, past French Senegal, stopping at British-controlled Sierra Leone, at Gold Coast ports, and at ports in the "Oil Rivers," as the Niger Delta was then known. Kingsley found that these places lived up to the vivid imaginary pictures of them she had formed from childhood reading. And the reality of West Africa tested the mettle of this eager, novice traveller: she weathered her first tornado, proving herself to be an able seaman; she felt the debilitating monotony of some of the coastal landscape; she came to an understanding of the psychological pressures on traders and officials who lived in such environments, isolated from contact with their fellows. Restricting herself to £300 in capital, Kingsley was quickly initiated into the life of a bush trader, travelling "very hard . . . tentless and living on native food and so on" and paying her way by "doing a little in rubber and ivory."[29] The African in his bush state became her companion, her trade adversary, and her friend. Although she confessed that she went to the West Coast expecting to dislike the "degraded, savage, cruel, brut[al]" African whose image filled the British press, she instead discovered not a stereotype but a human being, whom "on the whole" she liked (*TWA,* 653), especially when he had not been "corrupted" by the imported white culture. To a friend, she wrote: "I went far into the interior of the most dangerous part of all Africa, and I know the native well enough to be able to manage him with no white assistance . . . and I feel . . . he is not a bad sort of man."[30] With a keen eye for detail, Mary Kingsley recorded the dress, food, culture, architecture, and religion of various Africans she encountered, and with sympathetic understanding she tried to penetrate the "dark forest" of the African mind. Her empathy with the African sensibility, which took root on this first voyage, deepened on her second, longer trip and eventually blossomed into an impassioned defense in books, articles, and lectures on African culture.

In 1893 she finally disembarked at St. Paul Loanda in Portugese territory and made her way northward through the Congo Free State to the French Congo, ending her trek at British Old Calabar, from which she returned home in January 1894. In Old Calabar she befriended Sir Claude MacDonald, the High Commissioner of the Niger Coast Protectorate, whose wife was to be Kingsley's companion on her second voyage to Africa.

But, on this first trip, Kingsley generally avoided government circles; she formed her closest bonds, instead, with the "palm oil ruffians," or white traders, who educated her in the ways of the African, housed her, and provided her with access to remote interior regions where they had factories. Despite the negative public image created by their rough, immoral lives and their corruption of Africans through the liquor trade, the white traders—particularly kindred spirits like the amateur ethnologist R. E. Dennett—became Kingsley's close friends. Although she knew that she "ought to be shocked" by their behavior, she found that she was not, "because they were kind to me."[31] Back in England she confessed to feeling "lonely away from those men like Dennett and Parke. . . . They are my people, and their minds are like a print to me, whether they are drunk or sober, sick or well, bad or good. . . . I know how they think."[32] Her private letters give evidence that Miss Kingsley encountered the traders in all of the conditions she named, for she not only nursed several through bouts of fever but once saved the life of an inebriated British agent who had fallen headfirst into a water butt.

Clearly, Mary Kingsley felt a romantic attraction to the traders' rough, unconventional lives, to their courage and stamina in enduring loneliness and danger. With grim and exaggerated humor, tinged with an almost maternal solicitude, she tells a tall tale about the life of her friend, the trader MacTaggart: some Africans had "cut off the top of his head and grilled it the last time I had to nurse him: they had been making sauce out of his blood. . . . He is a most unfortunate man and a great worry to me."[33] Men like this seem the latter-day incarnations of Kingsley's heroes—the Drakes, the Hawkinses, the Hudsons of the Victorian era, who lived recklessly and preserved England's "honor" by extending her Empire.

But more than this, these men who lived on the fringes of civilization accepted and respected the shy, gawky, unconventional female traveller. In their world what you could do was the chief determinant of your worth. With them, too, Kingsley could enjoy an unrestrained social intercourse that would have been inconceivable in the staid drawing rooms at home. Perhaps because of her isolated childhood, perhaps because of her education and accent, Kingsley was intensely uncomfortable in conventional society and seemed to prefer saltier company. She once described escaping from the gentility of an afternoon call for "a carouse in the slums of Bristol in company with an ex-ship's carpenter and his wife and her sister, who plays divinely on the haircomb. . . ."[34] In a sense, the traders became a substitute family for Kingsley, offering her a comfortable identity as their caretaker, their champion, their "Aunt, a vexing, if even a valued, form of relative" (*WAS*, 311). Consciously and proudly, she identified herself as a trading man, "a Devil man . . . [who] must betray no weakness, but a character which I should describe as a compound of the best parts of . . . Cardinal Richlieu, Brutus, Julius Caesar, Prince Metternich, and Mettzofante" (*TWA*, 312). In private, she boasted to John Holt, head of a large Liverpool trading firm and a good friend, that she had been threatened by African traders "as to what would happen to me if I spoilt prices" in trading. A born trading man, however, Kingsley shocked several seasoned practitioners by her bargaining skills. When the agent of the Hatton and Cookson firm discovered the price she had paid for thirty pounds of rubber, he exclaimed: "Miss Kingsley, that I should ever live to see this day! You've been swindling those poor blacks!"[35]

The camaraderie that Kingsley developed with the traders on this first trip was to be a crucial force in the remaining eight years of her life, impelling her into the limelight after her second journey as spokeswoman for the interest of the merchants in the battle that raged over African territory and government in the final years of the 1890s. As duty to her family had first kept her at home and then sent her out to do her "father's work," so a newfound duty to her second family was to transform Mary Kingsley into a powerful polemist and a public personality.

The Second Trip

In less than a year Kingsley again returned to West Africa, this time for a more extended stay which was to provide the material for *Travels in West Africa* (1897) and *West African Studies* (1899). On 23 December 1894 she and Lady MacDonald boarded the *Batanga,* entrusting themselves to Kingsley's old friend, Captain Murray. As the ship made its way into the now-familiar ports on the Grain and Gold Coasts, she revelled in the spectacles provided by both man and nature. With a voracious appetite for factual information, an eye keenly sensitive to the "hum and buzz" of culture, and an irrepressible sense of humor, she recorded everything: geography; botany; colonial town planning, architecture, commerce; the strange habits of government officials; and the religion, appearance, craft, costume, and food of the Africans along the Coast.

Any summary of these travels pales before the actual narrative itself; however, a brief sketch of her path through Africa, illustrated by occasional passages from her two travel books, can give some indication of Kingsley's achievements both as a traveller and as a stylist.

The voyage on the *Batanga* terminated in Old Calabar, where Mary Kingsley spent four months with the MacDonalds "puddling about in river and forest," looking for fish, and visiting the Spanish-held island of Fernando Po in the Bight of Biafra. While in this region, Kingsley also made a pilgrimage to Okÿon to see a white woman whose missionary work had made her legendary, Mary Slessor. A former mill girl from Dundee who had lived for eighteen years at an isolated mission station, she was an authority on African culture, an arbiter of a number of disputes between local clans, and a crusader against practices like human sacrifice, ordeal by poison, and the murder of twins. The two Marys liked each other despite the differences in their religious beliefs. Kingsley valued Slessor's "knowledge of the native, his language, his ways of thought, his diseases, his difficulties, and all that is his," and she esteemed "the amount of good" that Miss Slessor had done (*TWA,* 74). The Scottish missionary was equally captivated by Kingsley's "sympathetic heart and fertile brain": "She had an individuality as pronounced as it was unique, with charm of manner and conversation, while the interplay of wit and mild satire, of pure spontaneous mirth and of profoundly deep seriousness, made her a series of surprises, each one tenderer and more surprising than the foregoing."[36]

The human contact may have been pleasant, but the fish specimens in the Oil Rivers area were disappointing. Kingsley longed to ascend the Niger River into the territory of the Royal Niger Company (RNC), from whose head, George Goldie, she had obtained assurances of assistance. However, in 1895 the government-controlled Niger Coast Protectorate and the RNC were at odds because of the company's restrictive trade policies, which had caused a rebellion among the inhabitants of the island of Brass. So, in order not to embarrass her host, Claude MacDonald, by travelling from his domain directly to Goldie's, Kingsley cancelled plans to fish the upper Niger. This initial experience of the political complexities and internecine rivalries on Africa's West Coast served as a prelude to her future involvement in African politics.

Because she wanted to collect fish from an equatorial river north of the Congo, Mary Kingsley travelled down to the French Congo and then ascended the Ogowé River. The experience of boarding a southbound steamer at the notoriously dangerous Lagos Bar proved to be a hilarious and trying experience in which passengers played "bob cherry" with sharks that hovered around the branch boats waiting to snap off a "stray" arm or leg. With characteristic irony, Kingsley observed that this transfer of people, chickens, ducks, and fish specimens "throws changing at Clapham Junction into the shade" (*TWA,* 76). After an uneventful voyage, Kingsley arrived at the harbor of Gaboon on 20 May 1895. At this time the French-controlled Congo encompassed a vast territory of 220,000 square miles with great unexplored stretches in the hinterlands, some of which Kingsley was to cross. Her passport for travel on the Ogowé was friendship with the agent general of Hatton and Cookson, whom she had met on her first voyage to the Coast and who got her passage on the firm's steamer, the *Mové.* Before departing on one of the most eventful segments of her journey, however, Kingsley paused at Gaboon to fish and talk with the pioneer explorer and writer about Africa, Dr. Robert Nassau.

On many of her voyages Kingsley kept an eclectic, vivid diary in which she recorded the physical and emotional impact of Africa. Her diary of the *Mové's* journey to Lembarene, which she quotes in her travel narrative, bristles with the vitality and drama of life on a trading ship as it sails past "grimly picturesque" landscape. At Lembarene she visited missionaries of the French Mission Évangélique, one of the few mission ventures she even remotely approved, and then boarded a paddle steamer, the *Éclaireur,* to travel further up the Ogowé to Talagouga. Again she stayed with cordial French missionaries whose personal charm and kindness she appreciated, although she disagreed with their proselytizing.

The forests, hills, and islands around Talagouga teemed with opportunities for solitary rambles or excursions by canoe, but Kingsley was still restless for great adventure—and more fish. Despite the concern of friends, she determined to explore the dangerous rapids on the Ogowé above Njole. Few Africans were willing to serve as crew on a journey into so perilous a land, and French officials were reluctant to allow a single white woman to travel into cannibal territory. But after demonstrating to them her competence and the superfluousness of male companionship, Mary Kingsley was allowed to continue on one of the adventures she later described as a "picnic."

In galvanic prose Kingsley captures every bump and jolt of her canoe during its journey through the rapids, where its inhabitants played "a knock-about farce, before King Death, in his amphi-theatre" (*TWA*, 191). As the theatrical metaphor indicates, how-ever, Kingsley distances herself and her readers from the hazards of the experience. Rather than inflating the dangers and aggran-dizing her own achievement, she renders life-threatening situa-tions in comic terms. The drama is entertaining, engrossing, but seldom terrifying. The kinetic narrative of this journey also reveals the traveller's keen sensitivity to beauty and her mystical propensities:

> The moon was rising, illumining the sky, but not yet sending down her light on the foaming, flying Ogowé in its deep ravine. The scene was divinely lovely; on every side out of the formless gloom rose the peaks of the Sierra del Cristal. . . . In the higher valleys where the dim light shone faintly, one could see wreaths and clouds of silver-gray mist lying, basking lazily or rolling to and fro. (*TWA*, 177)

As she stands in the "pool of utter night" with "thousands of fireflies" around her, Kingsley loses "all sense of human individ-uality, all memory of human life, with its grief and worry and doubt" (*TWA*, 177). She feels herself to be "part of the atmos-phere." Although raised by agnostics, Mary Kingsley had a deep, private faith in the world of the spirit; she embraced a pantheism that she identified as "firm African."

A less dangerous descent of the river returned the traveller to Talagouga and then to Lembarene, where she whiled away her time and provided "immense amusement" to her hosts by learning to paddle an Ogowé canoe. "There are only two things I am proud of," she later asserted, "one is that Doctor Günther has approved of my fishes, and the other is that I can paddle an Ogowé canoe, pace, style, steering and all . . . as if I were an Ogowé African" (*TWA*, 200). This achievement gave Kingsley a measure of independence and freedom: "I owe much of what I saw to having acquired the art of managing by myself a native canoe" (*TWA*, 196).

But the thrill of canoeing could not keep her at Lembarene for long. Soon she was planning a journey across largely unexplored land between the Ogowé and Rembwé rivers. Travelling through

territory populated by the cannibalistic Fan tribe with no government sanction or affiliation, Kingsley boldly ignored her own
danger. Occasionally, she confessed to an uncertainty about the
wisdom of her venture. For example, when told that her party
could not take the accustomed path because it was being held
by "those fearful Fans," Kingsley said that her hair began "to
rise" at memories of "what I have been told about those Fans and
the indications I have already seen of its being true. . . . Now
here we are going to try to get through the heart of their country,
far from a French station, and without the French flag. Why did
I not obey Mr. Hudson's orders not to go wandering about in
a reckless way! Anyhow I am in for it, and Fortune favors the
brave. The only question is: Do I individually come under this
class?" (*TWA*, 238). The danger was real but the tone of the
passage is not that of a frightened woman: the internal dialogue,
the mock plaint, and the final rhetorical question minimize the
sense of peril.

Despite her protestations of fear, Kingsley behaved with cool
courage in a number of potentially fatal situations on this journey.
When her party was given a threatening reception at a particularly
ominous village, Kingsley successfully played her role: "I got up
from my seat in the bottom of the canoe and leisurely strolled
ashore, saying to the line of angry faces 'M'boloani' in an un-
concerned way, although I well knew it was etiquette for them
to salute first. They grunted, but did not commit themselves
further" (*TWA*, 248). Soon after this performance, Kingsley and
her companions were allowed to enter the "exceedingly filthy"
village.

In each village Kingsley traded with the inhabitants, exchang-
ing cloth, fishhooks, tobacco, and sometimes even the clothes
on her back, for rubber, ivory, food, shelter, transportation, or
fish specimens. By her own testament she thrived on the "give-
and-take fun of bartering against their extortion" (*TWA*, 159).
In many places the "fun" was vitiated by the serious business of
doctoring villagers' severe wounds, infections, or parasitic diseases, and by encounters with the law. A few of her bearers
apparently had left a trail of broken debts, murders, and wife

"palavers" across the French Congo, and in several villages King-sley had to negotiate for their lives. As she told the Royal Scottish Geographical Society: "There is not a single crime that my three men were not taxed with having committed, and not only they themselves but their maternal ancestors. . . . I therefore used to have to stand hour after hour, dead tired with the day's march, wet through with its swamps and rivers, surrounded by sand flies and mosquitoes, pleading and arguing for their lives." Further-more she discovered that these porters, impressed by her forensic abilities, had purposely taken her to villages where they were wanted for crimes. In ironic tones, she expressed regret that she had "not allowed the village Fans just to nibble them slightly."[37]

Despite the trouble these bearers gave her, Kingsley found them entertaining, intriguing company. As if they were char-acters in a comedy of humors, Kingsley named the men according to their salient personal or sartorial characteristics: the Ajumba tribesmen were styled "Gray Shirt," "Singlet," "Pagan," and "Silence," an unpaid camp follower of imposing manner, "the Duke." The Fans who joined her party—Kiva, Wiki, and Fika— became valued companions during the trek through rugged ter-rain where courage and physical stamina were essential to survival: "A certain sort of friendship soon arose between the Fans and me. We each recognized that we belonged to that same section of the human race with whom it is better to drink than to fight. We knew we would each have killed the other, if sufficient induce-ment were offered, and so we took a certain amount of care that the inducement should not arise" (*TWA*, 264).

Her adventurous journey with these fierce companions ended at Agonjo on the Rembwé, where Kingsley bade "a touching farewell" to the Africans with whom she had endured so much. However, she had only a few days to miss her "friends" before another compelling black man came into her life—an African bush trader named Obanjo, who served as her pilot downriver to Glass. An incarnation of the buccaneer spirit she so admired, the theatrical Obanjo comes vividly to life in her narrative: "He used to look covertly at you every now and then to see if he had produced his impression, which was evidently intended to be that of a reckless, rollicking skipper. There was a Hallo-my-Hearty atmosphere coming off him from the top of his hat to the soles of his feet, like the scent off a flower" (*TWA*, 335). Kingsley added that, if she ever desired a "wild and awful" career in West Africa, she would choose Obanjo as her companion because he was a man "whom I could rely on, that if . . . [we] went into the utter bush together, one of us at least would come out alive" (*TWA*, 335). Although they did not flee to the "utter bush" together, the pair did fight off an attack by an armed party of Fans. Obanjo even trusted Kingsley to navigate at night while he slept. The solitary communion with nature on these evenings enchanted Kingsley, the pantheist, who admired the pathway of "frosted silver" created by the moonlight in the center of "the great, black, winding river" and marvelled at the "ink-black mangrove walls" bordering the river "and above them the band of star and moonlit heavens that the walls of mangrove allowed one to see" (*TWA*, 338). But this downriver journey was apparently a good bit more raucous than Mary Kingsley publicly admitted. To Lady MacDonald, she admitted that she had exercised "much care" in writing this section of the travels, "for I consorted while on that forsaken River with bold black traders—and we . . . used to stay every night at a village and have 'chatty' little times owing to my black companions . . . going in heavily for rum."[38] Clearly, Kingsley was not only a good sailor and a fine trader but an excellent companion, for, at the journey's end, Obanjo tried to persuade her to join him in a trading venture "up another river, a notorious river, in the neighbouring Spanish territory" (*TWA*, 348). Reluctantly she declined this invitation on an excursion that promised, as she wryly observed, to be "rich in incident and highly interesting" (*TWA*, 349). She lingered instead in the tamer environs of Glass, discussing African religion with Dr. Nassau and visiting the island of Corisco to watch the yearly fishing done by the women and to collect specimens.

The final leg of this second journey took Kingsley from Glass to the German territory around the mouth of the Cameroon River. An avid reader of mountaineering books, though not a climber herself, Kingsley there confronted her "great temptation—the

magnificent Mungo Mah Lobeh—the Throne of Thunder"
(*TWA,* 549). This 13,760-foot mountain with its commanding
view had previously been scaled by two Englishmen, one of whom
was Kingsley's hero, Richard Burton. An inexperienced moun-
taineer with no equipment, this lady traveller nonetheless decided
to ascend the southeast face of Mungo, an approach that had been
used only once before by a party of German officers. Motivated
by a lust for adventure and perhaps even for some personal glory,
Kingsley began the arduous climb in the rainy season—an undertaking which sorely tested her physical stamina and psychological strength. The seasonal fog, cold, and rain were debilitating.
Her African bearers, fearful of the dangers, tried continually to
sabotage the climb in order to force her to turn back. Kingsley
had to quell the rebellion, organize the camp, inspirit her African
companions, and muster the energy to propel herself up the slope.
Finally, short of food and water, exhausted and depressed, with
a face flayed and bloody, she reached the summit—only to find
that the weather had "robbed" her of her view. Stifling her
disappointment, Kingsley left a characteristically tongue-in-
cheek monument to her achievement: her calling card, placed
next to the celebratory champagne bottles of the German climb-
ers. But she was proud of her accomplishment. Writing to Macmillan on 23 July 1897, Kingsley boasted: "I find from the
Germans that I am not the second but the first to go up Mungo
the way I went." The only public self-congratulation she allowed
herself, however, was an expression of satisfaction at having "got
my men up so high, and back again, undamaged; . . . as they
said, I was a Father and a Mother to them, and a very stern
though kind set of parents I have been" (*TWA,* 604).

This anticlimactic ascent capped Kingsley's extraordinary journey. In November 1895 she boarded the homeward-bound *Batanga.* And even before the ship docked in Liverpool this obscure
woman traveller had become a sort of celebrity; she wrote to
Macmillan on her voyage home, expressing "disgust and alarm"
about the accounts of her exploits that had appeared in the papers
and voicing fear that her travels and opinions were being exaggerated and distorted.[39] Her father's friend, Dr. Guillemard,

wrote teasingly about her growing reputation: "I am quite a distinguished person here because I am a friend of Mary Kingsley. I entertain the dinner-table with anecdotes, how you invariably travel disguised as an arab shiek and generally have a well-hung leg in your portmanteau—your special object in visiting Africa being to report on the suitability of man as an article of *diet*."[40] Kingsley herself parodied the kind of notices that appeared in the American press: "Miss Kingsley, having crossed the continent of Africa, ascended the Niger to Victoria, and then climbed the Peak of Cameroon . . . [will] return to England, where she will deliver a series of lectures on French art, which she has had great opportunities of studying" (*WAS*, vii).

Sometimes, however, newspaper assertions could not be jokingly dismissed. When the *Daily Telegraph* (13 November 1895), praising her for having "manfully" endured the perils of travel, styled her a "new woman," Kingsley immediately wrote the paper to deny the charge. Similarly, when the *Spectator* (7 December 1895), writing on "The Negro Future," asserted that the accounts of Miss Kingsley's adventures "brought to mind the question 'What makes the African continent so bad?' and why are the African people so 'abnormally low, evil, cruel'?" Kingsley was forced to join battle. She sent the paper a firm denial of the opinions attributed to her and launched upon a campaign of public education and self-vindication that was to engross her for the five years that remained of her life. She took to the podium, addressing geographical, anthropological, and missionary societies, as well as college students, Eton boys, and trading associations. Mary Kingsley was on her way to becoming, in Stephen Gwynn's words, "the most effective propagandist of her time."[41]

The Controversies, 1895–1897:
Missionaries, Traders, and Africans

Within four months of her return to England, Mary Kingsley had plunged herself into the heart of several momentous controversies about Africa and Africans. In articles published in leading journals, she advanced her views on the prevailing misconceptions of Africans, the failure of missionary efforts, the complexity of

African tribal culture, and the good done by white traders. The first of these pieces, "The Development of Dodos" (*National Review*, March 1896), presents in embryonic form the major arguments that Kingsley developed and articulated throughout her public career. It opens with an ironic parable attacking attitudes toward Africans:

> There was once upon a time a certain country, and in this country lived birds called Dodos. Many excellent ladies and gentlemen heard of them, and from what they heard they feared the birds were not in a satisfactory spiritual state. . . . When they came to the Dodos and found how very patient and cheerful . . . the birds were, they called this state of mind "childlike," and said, "My dear Dodos, you are very sweet, you are our Brethern, and all you have got to do is to learn to sing hymns, and put on some Hubbards [dresses] and trousers, and then you will be perfect gems quite as good as we are." (66)

Here Kingsley ridicules erroneous ideas about the "childishness" of Africans and their "arrested" psychological, intellectual, and moral development. She also parodies the missionary's eagerness to transform Africans into Christians in European garb and the assumption that such a metamorphosis will necessarily advance black people on the ladder of civilization. Missionaries' attempts to extirpate immoral African practices and to Christianize the heathens are, in Kingsley's view, efforts to destroy African culture. She remarks ironically that Africans, unlike Dodos, have not become extinct because "the whole flock have not strictly attended to all they have been told" by white men (66). Kingsley also disputes the missionary's conception of the African as "an undeveloped European," a brother who could easily be made to share a European point of view. A believer in human polygenesis—the simultaneous existence of several Edens from which various races emerge—she argues that Africans are totally different in kind from white men; their outlook on life is chiefly "spiritual" while that of the European is "materialistic." Africans are, then, an inferior race not because they are heathens but because they lack mechanical aptitude and the drive to advance technologically that has marked the history of Western Europe.

Thus Kingsley's own attitudes toward Africans are complex: she respects their culture and deplores its corruption by a "rubbishy white culture" which is undermining African institutions, yet she sees African civilization as radically different from and inferior—"in degree not kind"—to Western civilization. British by birth and an imperialist at heart, Kingsley nonetheless identifies herself as "a firm African" in religion and befriends the least Westernized Africans she encounters, the cannibalistic Fans, because "they are brave and so you can respect them. . . . They are on the whole a fine race" (*TWA*, 328).

Like M. A. Pringle, Mary Kingsley blames the cultural chauvinism of missionaries for the failure of many mission ventures. She berates "their tendency to regard the African minds as so many jugs, which have only to be emptied . . . and refilled with the particular form of doctrine . . . the missionaries are engaged in teaching" ("The Development of Dodos," 69). This attitude and the behavior it engenders are responsible for the failures that missionaries blame on the liquor traffic, polygamy, and heathenism. Moreover, by Christianizing Africans and severing their vital links with tribal traditions and customs, missionaries create a culturally and morally rootless people to whom they can offer nothing substantive. Mission schools, according to Mary Kingsley, fail to teach Africans truly useful skills; girls, destined to live in huts where "household linen is non-existant," are taught to wash and mend, while boys are trained to be clerks in white firms—jobs for which the supply of labor already exceeds the demand. Although she befriended individual missionaries and praised the efforts of the Mission Évangélique, Mary Kingsley opposed the assumptions behind all missionary activity and allied herself with the "devil's party," the West African traders.

The traders and missionaries perceived each other as enemies. Kingsley bluntly acknowledged that she often longed "to wring the neck of the . . . male missionary, when he starts telling me 'things I really ought to know' about my friend the local trader" ("The Development of Dodos," 74). Having travelled through Africa herself as a "trading man," she respected and felt a kinship with the traders whose bad reputations she tried to rehabilitate in her writings. For example, in order to disprove the missionary's claim that the trader's sale of liquor to the African was turning him into a "habitual drunkard," Kingsley draws a striking cultural parallel: "I have no hesitation in saying that in the whole of West Africa, in one week, there is not one-quarter the amount of drunkenness you can see any Saturday night . . . in Vauxhall Road" (*TWA*, 663). She even had samples of trade gin chemically analyzed to prove that it was not poisonous. This defense of the liquor trade manifests not only Kingsley's affection for the white traders but also her conviction of the importance of trade to the British Empire. An "old-fashioned imperialist," Kinglsey believed that the "life blood of England is her trade" (*WAS*, 255) and that empire inevitably follows trade; she would have agreed with Lord Palmerston that Providence had decreed "that commerce may go freely forth, leading civilization with one hand, and peace with the other to render mankind happier, wiser, better."[42] That Britain had a right to amass territory throughout the world and that her country ought continually to seek new markets for its manufactured goods were two unshakable tenets of Kingsley's creed. To her mind, traders in West Africa served their nation by obtaining raw materials from, and selling British manufactures to, Africans.

According to Kingsley, traders understand Africans far better than do missionaries; indeed, the "palm oil ruffians" are uniquely committed to maintaining the peace and prosperity of Africans and to preserving African culture from the adulterations of civilization. The traders can see the "real African" in a way that missionaries, blinded by their religious commitment and their cultural prejudices, cannot. As both a "trading man" and an ethnologist, Mary Kingsley perceives the logic, the social necessity, and the religious significance of many African practices. As a human being, she finds that the melancholy and the spiritual orientation of an African's personality resonates with her own. She, therefore, urges readers of her first article to put themselves in the West African's place, to see polygamy, spirit worship, and cannibalism through his eyes, as pieces of his cultural fabric.

"The Development of Dodos," the first salvo in Kingsley's campaign to educate British readers about Africans and the political realities of Africa, was followed four months later by "Black Ghosts" (*Cornhill,* July 1896). Prefaced by a long, humorous digression on the author's own experiences with European ghosts, this article integrates scholarly observation with amusing narrative in a way that foreshadows Kingsley's technique in her two books. In content, too, this piece anticipates *Travels in West Africa* (1897) and *West African Studies* (1899) by its careful documentation of African religion, its comparison of African attitudes toward spirits with those held by a revered figure like the Victorian Poet Laureate Alfred Lord Tennyson, and by its contention that African religious beliefs and practices are "consistent and logical" (82).

As her letters during the year after her return make clear, Kingsley was eager both to promulgate her special knowledge of Africans and to keep herself before the public eye. She told Macmillan that she had accepted so many invitations to speak and write because of her "commercial instinct": "if I had not done so I should have been forgotten by now" (6 July 1896). In 1897, while she was also working on the manuscript of her first book, Kingsley produced five articles, all of which present valuable anthropological information in the context of sprightly, amusing narrative. "Fishing in West Africa" (*National Review,* May 1897) humorously depicts the mishaps that befall the narrator, who calls herself "a born poacher," as she searches for fish for her collection. "Two African Days' Entertainment" (*Cornhill,* March 1897) continues in the same lighthearted vein by recounting Kingsley's "entertaining" ministrations to a man suffering from brain fever and to a dog thought to be hydrophobic. This article not only provides some insight into African medical practices, it also sketches the outline of a persona that Kingsley fleshes out more completely in her books: a self-mocking woman who is both competent and ludicrously inept: a persona who, frightened "out of . . . [her] wits" by the convulsions of her patient, drops her scissors and "rear[s], driving my head up through the roof, and tearing that structure from its supports" (356). This self-mocking narrator adds that she wore the roof "as a collar or neck-ruff " (356). An equally amusing persona narrates a digressive African folk tale in "A Parrot Story" (*Cornhill,* September 1897); the tale illustrates the religion and the family relationships prevalent in Africa while also revealing the narrator's own fascination with Africa: "One of the charms of studying in West Africa is the keen human interest that comes off every mortal subject like the scent off a flower" (389). More scholarly but nonetheless entertaining are "African Religion and Law" (*National Review,* September 1897), an analysis of the religious basis of many African legal institutions, and "The Fetish View of the Human Soul" (*Folklore,* June 1897), an examination of the animistic religious beliefs of West African tribes.

Writing the Travels

As early as August 1894, after her return from Africa, Mary Kingsley was planning a narrative of her adventures. She wrote at that time to the Macmillan firm, the publishers of her father's and uncle's works, to inquire if they would be interested in her travel journals. Before she left England for her second African journey, she seems to have sent Macmillan some narrative of her experiences, a production which she deprecatingly described as "well-intentioned word-swamps" (18 December 1894). Her numerous lectures and articles of 1896 and 1897 not only tested the public response to her ideas, they also helped her to overcome some of her misgivings about her ability to write clear, grammatical prose. Lacking formal education, not to mention formal training as an ethnologist, Kingsley felt inadequate to the task of writing about her experiences and observations. Thus, she corresponded with authorities on the West Coast of Africa, read extensively in the existing ethnographic and travel literature, and asked scientific friends like Dr. Guillemard to edit her manuscript. In the Preface to *Travels in West Africa,* Kingsley anxiously assures her audience that they are about to read a scientifically accurate book: "I beg to state that I have written only on things that I know from personal experience and very careful observation. I have never accepted an explanation of a native custom from one person alone nor have I set down things as being prevalent customs from having seen a single instance" (*TWA,* xxii). Like other lady travellers, Kingsley felt a special need to vouch for her factual accuracy and to dispel any prejudices about her objectivity. As a result, occasionally, she omitted aspects of West Africa that she did not feel competent to discuss from extensive personal experience. She avoided discussing the Oil Rivers in her first book because "I do not feel that I yet know enough to have the right to speak regarding them, unless I were going to do so along accepted, well-trodden lines, and what I have seen and personally know of the region does not make me feel at all inclined to do this" (*TWA,* 73). On several occasions she even found that her empirical observations contradicted the theories of anthropological luminaries like J. G. Frazer and E. B. Tylor; thus she had to be extremely careful to establish the accuracy of her views. In addition, despite the obvious advantage to having maps in a travel book, Kingsley refused to condone the inclusion of maps in *Travels in West Africa* because, as she told Macmillan, "I don't want to assert without giving lats. and longs. [*sic*] that I traversed hundreds of miles in various districts never before traversed by whites" (17 August 1897). Such illogical reasoning betrays Kingsley's fear—which sometimes borders on obsession—of being caught in an inaccuracy which would discredit her work.

Not only was Kingsley concerned about the methodological problems of studying the multifarious, sometimes baffling cultures of West Africa, she was also haunted by fear of her inability to construct an orderly, entertaining narrative out of her chaotic journals. Jokingly, she offers the contents of her bush diary as an example of both the complexity of Africa and her own disorganization: "My notes for a day will contain facts relating to the kraw-kraw, price of onions, size and number of fish caught, cooking recipes, genealogies, oaths (native form of), law cases, and market prices" (*TWA,* 73). Her letters to Macmillan during the composition of her first book indicate bewilderment about the form that her work should take.[43] In 1896 she seems to have been planning two books: one, a travel narrative written with "an eye to the English public," to be published in summer for "light reading" (13 May 1896); another, a scientific work directed to a scholarly audience at home and to friends in West Africa, which would be published in the winter. About the travel narrative Kingsley was flippant, suggesting that it be called "the log of a lighthearted lunatic" (11 December 1895), but she was anxious to write a popular, money-making book (21 November 1895). She even worried that publication delays had caused her work to "overstay . . . its market" (2 January 1895). About her scientific book she was intensely serious, yet she acknowledged to Macmillan in 1896 that the fate of her scholarly work was inextricably tied to that of the more popular travel account. The problem of melding scientific writing and personal narrative was partially resolved in 1897 by *Travels in West Africa,* a work which derives its structure from Kingsley's journey and describes many of her adventures but which also includes ethnological data and an extensive scholarly appendix on West African trade, labor, disease, reptiles, and fish. Two years after its appearance, Kingsley published a more scholarly volume, *West African Studies,* that incorporates much of the ethnological material "crowded out" of *Travels in West Africa;* yet even this work is not scientifically impersonal, for it begins with a raucous narrative of life on a West Coast steamer—a chapter that Kingsley excised from her first book because friends found it "to racy."

Kingsley worried not only about the shape and accuracy of her narrative but also about its style. Apologizing for the shortcomings of her "word-swamps," she prefaces each of her books with avowals that she is not "a literary man," only an untutored recorder of facts and experiences. Just as her use of the metaphor, "word-swamp," belies her disclaimer of verbal skill, so her self-deprecating prefaces serve an important rhetorical function. Like the *exordia,* the formal introductions of classical orations, they win the reader over to the side of the struggling, honest, plainspeaking narrator while also engendering curiosity about the nature of the book. Kingsley's ambivalent attitude toward her own prose is evident in her responses to the editing of *Travels in West Africa.* Although she sought and received help from friends like Lucy Toulmin-Smith and Dr. Guillemard, she balked at the latter's attempt to straitjacket her writing into a more concise, scientific, latinate prose. After reading some proofs of *Travels* that Guillemard had corrected, she wrote to her father's friend with a combination of self-deprecation and self-assertion:

I clearly see that the book has not got in it enough original literary merit for you to work on. Your corrections stand on stilts out of the swamps and give a very quaint but patchy aspect to the affair, so that I do not know my way about it at all. I never meant you to take this detail labour over the thing, but only to arrange it and tell me point-blank if I was lying about scientific subjects. I would rather have the rest of the stuff published as it stands.[44]

The apologetic tone here cannot completely mask Kingsley's resolve that the style of the book should be absolutely and recognizably her own. In fact, she insisted that Macmillan allow her to approve all of Guillemard's changes before they were incorporated (26 September 1896). Later, after the successful reception of her first book, Kingsley told an aspiring writer: "I am popular because I am natural."[45] And she wrote to Macmillan (n.d.) that the public enthusiasm for her writing showed that "there must be some people who care for things as they are, with all the go and glory and beauty in them as well as the mechanism and the microbes."[46]

Rhythmical, powerfully descriptive, allusive, metaphorical, Kingsley's prose in her articles and in both books captures the "go, glory, and beauty" of West Africa. A sympathetic observer of nature, Kingsley could record the color and detail of a landscape without falling into the cloyingly studied or bombastic prose of the amateur naturalist. For example, both the sights and the emotional ambience of a night journey on the Ogowé are rendered in this description:

The moonlit sea, shimmering and breaking on the darkened shore, the black forest and the hills silhouetted against the star-powdered purple sky, and, at my feet, the engine-room stoke-hole, lit with the rose-coloured glow from its furnace, showing by the great wood fire the two nearly naked Krumen stokers, shining like polished bronze in their perspiration, as they throw in on to the fire the billets of red wood that look like freshly-cut chunks of flesh." (*TWA*, 124)

A discrete moment on a particular river epitomizes the character of West Africa, a place where savagery and incredible beauty go hand-in-hand. The metaphors here have a special potency because French West Africa, the home of the cannibalistic tribes, is a place where the imagination's wildest and most terrifying fantasies are, indeed, actualities.

Like Joseph Conrad, whose *Nigger of the Narcissus* she admired, Kingsley knew the psychological malaise that can destroy white men in Africa and the chtonian forces that lurk in the jungle. She warned that the study of African forms of thought could be "bad for the brain" when pursued in the "often unaccountable surroundings, and depressing scenery of the Land of the Shadow of Death" (*TWA*, 441). She also knew that "your own mind requires protection when you send it stalking the savage idea through the tangled forests, dark caves, the swamps and fogs of the Ethiopian intellect" (*TWA*, 440). Although she was never overwhelmed by the "horror" than engulfed Conrad's Kurtz in West Africa, Kingsley nonetheless experienced the psychic perils of that land and depicted the eerie, ominous landscape in a way that anticipates Marlow in the *Heart of Darkness*. In that story, Marlow tells his audience about travelling upriver on a Kadina steamer: "in and out of rivers, streams of death in life, whose banks were rotting into mud, whose waters thickened into slime, invaded the contorted mangroves, that seemed to writhe at us in the extremity of an impotent despair. . . . The general sense of vague and oppressive wonder grew upon me. It was like a weary pilgrimage amongst hints for nightmares."[47] Two years before this was written, Mary Kingsley also tried to capture the quintessence of these swamps in an allusive, metaphoric prose. For Kingsley this is a kingdom of death traversed by a Styx-like river smelling of the "black batter-like stinking slime" (*TWA*, 89) and surrounded by monotonous walls of mangrove: "unvarying in color, unvarying in form, unvarying in height" (*TWA*, 96). In this primordial world human life and time become irrelevant; man is but another potential fossil. Here danger is palpable. Even the smell of the malarial mud becomes incarnate, "creeping and crawling and gliding out from the side creeks, and between mangrove-roots, laying itself upon the river, stretching and rolling in a kind of grim play, and finally crawling up the side of the ship to come on board and leave its cloak of moisture" (*TWA*, 96). The repeated participles here mimic the slow but inexorable advance of the odor; moreover, the description itself attests to the nightmarish quality of all perceptions in this depressing and disorienting landscape. But like Marlow, Kingsley is not so much repelled by the swamps as strangely fascinated by their grotesque other-worldiness and their incomprehensible allure.

For late nineteenth-century novelists like H. Rider Haggard and Joseph Conrad, the journey through Africa often served as a metaphor for a psychological voyage into the "unknown regions of oneself, the unconscious" where the traveller encounters the primal "dangers and splendors of the human condition."[48] This motif plays a minor but significant part in Kingsley's writings. As she admitted to her readers, the journal of an isolated white person in the interior of Africa would undoubtedly provide "exceedingly interesting" material for "psychological study" (*TWA*, 101). However, since her focus is not on psychology but "on the state of things in general in West Africa" (*TWA*, 101), Kingsley purposely excluded her journal entries—or used only such facts as enhance a narrative structured consciously to appeal to "the general reader." Since journal entries distort experience by leaving the reader with a vivid impression of relatively minor events but little sense of the meaning of the whole, Kingsley restricted herself to a limited use of these immediate records of her experiences. The public aims of the narrative—education and entertainment—took precedence over the exploration of the private meaning of the travels.

However, the metaphors and the language that Kingsley employs do betray some of the personal psychological significance of her travels. The journey into "the great, grim twilight regions of the forest" (*TWA*, 101) seems a spiritual progress toward an "enlightened" state. When she first embarks, the traveller is virtually blind to what surrounds her; metaphorically she is an illiterate in a vast, rich library. In this preliminary stage she realizes the extent of her dependence on other people or on familiar surroundings and is forced to turn inward to discover in herself the resources to deal with this new condition. Gradually, the voyager learns to see anew: "inextricable tangles" of vegetation resolve themselves into almost preternatural clearness and "a whole world grows up out of the gloom" (*TWA*, 101). In this "illumined" state, the tyro feels "a sense of growing power," which climaxes in a conviction of invincibility: "Put me where you like in an African forest, and as far as the forest goes, starve me or kill me if you can" (*TWA*, 103). If Conrad's Marlow or Haggard's Alan Quartermain found in Africa's hinterlands the bestiality at the center of all men's hearts,[49] Mary Kingsley discovered something different: the power and self-sufficiency of the African "natural man" which were available to a white woman too if she left behind the restraints and dependencies of the "civilized" world. But the journey through Africa also brought Kingsley a second enlightenment: a knowledge of African peoples that was simultaneously a new self-knowledge. Just as she learned to see anew in the African forest, she gained insight into the African mind and in so doing realized: "I am a firm African."[50]

Kingsley's metaphors reveal her close identification with the land and the inhabitants of Africa; her frequent literary and artistic allusions manifest her desire to make the reader, too, identify with this strange and distant world. References to her favorite authors—Dickens, Stevenson, Kipling—or to Twain, Dr. Johnson, Goethe, and the Bible help to bring Africa into an understandable frame of reference for the reader. Similarly, alien, unimaginable scenery is made accessible to the Victorian public through comparison with paintings by Turner, G. F. Watts, or the Pre-Raphaelites. In addition, the "choruses" and "symphonies" of Africa become audible to the armchair traveller when they are compared to the music of Beethoven, Handel, or those Victorian favorites, Gilbert and Sullivan. By familiarizing the exotic and frightening, Kingsley encourages her readers to delight in West Africa as she does.

Despite her claims to the contrary, then, Kingsley's prose style is complex and highly literate. In fact, her chatty, digressive, witty narrative voice traces its antecedents to the travel writers and novelists of the eighteenth century: "I am convinced," she observed, "that I have somehow strayed out of the eighteenth century into modern life. . . . My style and that of the early navigators is one and the same."[51] The chapter headings of *Travels in West Africa,* for example, employ a tongue-in-cheek tone and an irony reminiscent of Fielding's chapter headings in *Tom Jones* or *Joseph Andrews:*

Chapter XVIII
From Corisco to Gaboon
The log of the *Lafayette* on her return voyage . . . giving some account of Cape Esterias and the inhabitants thereof; to which is added a full and particular account of a strange sailing manoeuvre, first carried out by this voyager, and not included in any published treatise on the art of seamanship in the known world. (*TWA,* 410)

In these headings and throughout the narrative, the "Voyager" is depicted as a kind of picaresque hero[52] moving through a world of strange and marvellous adventure. Like the classic picaro, Kingsley, the outsider, "fits" in no one social context but moves easily through a number of diverse situations: from the homes of colonial government officials, to the outposts of missions, to the rugged, all-male "bush" stations of traders, to cannibalistic villages, to lone safaris through hostile territory. Her adventures are presented in a digressive, episodic structure and are narrated in baroque, or loose, sentences like the following:

Into that tree the canoe shot with a crash, and I hung on, and shipping my paddle, pulled the canoe into the slack water again, by the aid of the branches of the tree, which I was in mortal terror would come off the rock, and insist on accompanying me and the canoe, via Kama country, to the Atlantic Ocean; but it held, and when I had got safe against the side of the pinnacle-rock I wiped a perspiring brow, and searched in my mind for a piece of information regarding navigation that would be applicable to the management of long-tailed Adooma canoes. (*TWA,* 198)

Beginning with the main idea, this sentence piles on successive phrases, clauses, and parenthetical expressions, suggesting by its lack of grammatical parallelism and its length "a speaker in the process of improvising his thoughts."[53] Sometimes, the narrator of these travels, sounding like Sterne in *Tristram Shandy*, confesses a mock-dismay at her inability to order the flow of the narrative or to repress shocking details; moreover, she invites readers to witness the amusing spectacle of her mind at work:

> But I must forthwith stop writing about the Gold Coast, or I shall go on telling you stories and wasting your time, not to mention the danger of letting out those which would damage the nerves of the cultured of temperate climes, such as . . . the moving story of three leeches and two gentlemen; . . . and the reason why you should not eat pork along here because all the natives have either got the guinea-worm, or kraw-kraw or ulcers; and then the pigs go and—dear me! it was a near thing that time. I'll leave off at once. (*TWA*, 41)

This celebration of the digressiveness of the narrative and Kingsley's warning that *Travels in West Africa* "has no pretension to being a connected work" (*TWA*, 42) indicate that Kingsley perceived her journey not as a quest but as what MacLulich calls an "odyssey."[54] Like the Canadian explorers whose "odysseys" he studied, Kingsley focused her narrative on the incidental details of her journey and surrendered herself to the novel experiences afforded by travel. According to MacLulich, travellers who perceive their journeys as quest-romances "cling to the values of their society of origin, and seek to impose themselves and their purposes on both their own subordinates and the native peopes they encounter. In contrast, an odyssean explorer adapts to the non-European conditions with which he is surrounded; his account depicts a learning process analogous to the education or initiation undergone by the central characters of many novels."[55] Kingsley revealed her "odyssean" approach to travel in a letter to Lady MacDonald in which she distinguished herself from the typical nineteenth-century African traveller, a "peculiar sort of animal only capable of seeing a certain set of things and always seeing them the same way."[56] Unlike this "animal," Kingsley is a traveller who relishes the serendipity of a journey through Africa. As she joked to Lady MacDonald: "I've come to the decision that it is the greatest mistake to write a book about a place you have been to . . . for personal experiences get in your way sadly."[57]

In a buoyant, immediate prose, Kingsley often draws her readers into those experiences, treating them as companions who participate with her in the initiation into Africa's mysteries. When the action is exciting, Kingsley shifts from past-tense narrative to a present-tense diary so that readers feel the immediacy and the excitement of dramatic moments. On other occasions, the narrator directly addresses her audience, forestalls their objections, and tries to carry her point by a joke or an apt analogy. For example, anticipating that readers may be skeptical about her claim that Africans continue to believe in a god even if he fails to answer their prayers, the narrator challenges: "You white men will say, 'Why go on believing in him then?' But that is an idea that does not enter the African mind. I might just as well say 'Why do you go on believing in . . . hansom cabs,' because one . . . driver malignantly fails to take you where you want to go, or fails to arrive in time. . . ." (*TWA*, 506).

Kingsley sought to win her audience's full attention and to garner their favor because of the unique book she was writing: a travel narrative aimed at a popular audience which was also a scientific work directed at a more professional readership and a political document designed to change the attitudes of the public as well as of colonial administrators. Her editing of *Travels in West Africa* indicates Kingsley's awareness of the diverse audiences she was trying to address. She wrote repeatedly to Macmillan about her attempts to verify every scientific observation in the book, and she resisted any editing that would raise questions about her credibility: "I have no character to lose as a literary person but I have got a good character to lose as a practical sea man and an honest observer of facts on the West Coast."[58] She even omitted experiences so sensational that they might cause readers to be skeptical about her honesty. For example, she excised from her writings the description of an extremely close encounter with a gorilla about which she told Stephen Gwynn and his guests over tea: " 'the nearest I ever was to a gorilla . . . was when I was up in the bush with some cannibal Fans. . . .' The male stood there roaring and advanced, 'I asked the Fan beside me if he had not better shoot' she said, 'for he [the gorilla] was looking very nasty.' 'I must wait,' he said; 'the other man's powder is wet.' So he waited till the muzzle almost touched, and then blew the creature's chest in."[59] Gwynn goes on in this same passage to note that Kingsley's account of her cool courage in this instance caused one of his guests to drop her teacup and to question the sanity of the prim lady narrator. Given this auditor's response, perhaps Kingsley was wise in excluding mention of the time she sprang from her canoe to chase an armed African who had fired at her, or the time she freed a leopard from its cage, or the time she was flung out of her boat into a river filled with hungry crocodiles. Such hair-raising incidents would not only focus undue attention on the personal qualities of the explorer—an unladylike thing to do—but might also jeopardize her reputation as a reliable observer.

Kingsley also was careful to edit out of her book "all the poetry and bad language except for the native legal oaths"[60] in order not to scandalize her public. She admitted to Lady MacDonald that:

the amount of expurgation my journals have required has been awful. My well-known veneration for Governors, Consul-Generals, and Bishops has necessitated much crossing out. . . . I have had to entirely eliminate a lovely scene in the Ogowé, when I and the captain of a vessel had to take to the saloon table because a Bishop with a long red beard and voluminous white flannel petticoats was rolling about the floor in close but warful embrace with the Governor of the Ogowé.[61]

The grimly humorous narrative of her voyage down the Coast in the company of the macabre Old Coasters was left out of her first book because it offended friends and might alienate readers (it later appeared as the introductory chapter of *West African Studies*). Possibly because she did not want to make herself seem heroic or possibly because she feared that she would damage her reputation as a lady if she talked about nights spent alone in the bush with white men—even delirious white men—Kingsley omitted several of her experiences nursing yellow fever victims and sick or drunken traders. Thus, although Dr. Guillemard late in his life accused Kingsley of having exaggerated some of her adventures and of having been carried away "by a tidal wave of words,"[62] it does seem that, in general, she tried to avoid such exaggerations in her two books, selecting materials that would inform and entertain her readers without ever alienating them.

Kingsley's consciousness of the need to address a diverse public, with differing expectations of a travel book, led her to assume several different personae in her writing—serious scholar, rakish adventurer, naive but lucky traveller, clown, and prim Victorian lady. In her attempt to accommodate the demands of her material to the capabilities of her audience, while at the same time meeting the exigencies of personal psychological needs, Kingsley produced a remarkable, multifaceted book: a scientific tract with an engaging plot line, a travel book with the weight of a scholarly treatise, and a political document that is disarmingly like a picaresque novel.

Humor

Kingsley's literary sophistication is perhaps most evident in the range of her humor: slapstick, parody, verbal irony, satire, black humor, and mock heroic humor can all be found in her articles and books. In fact, the *Evening News* observed that both of her books were rich "in that quality in which the writings of women seldom excel: the divine quality of humor."[63] Her readings of Dickens and Mark Twain, two of her favorite authors, seem to have given her the key to one of the fundamental principles of comic contradiction: "the operation of physical laws upon inorganic objects . . . in such a way that it is they who appear to be acting from personal volition" while the human being becomes "the passive thing."[64] This technique is evident in her account of a government official who becomes the victim of a defective piece of string at the waist of his Turkish trousers: "He writes furiously—blotting paper mislaid—frantic flurry round—pantaloons won't stand it—grab just saves them—something wanted the other side of the room—headlong flight towards it—'now's our chance,' think the pantaloons, and make off— recaptured" (*TWA*, 110).

In another case, the speaker herself is the victim of an African bush rope which impedes her progress down the mountain: "It festoons itself from tree to tree, and when your mind is set on other things, catches you under the chin, and gives you the appearance of having made a determined but ineffectual attempt to cut your throat with a saw. It whisks off your hat and grabs your clothes, and commits other iniquities too numerous to catalogue here" (*TWA*, 601). Inanimate objects frequently take on human characteristics in *Travels in West Africa*, perhaps because Mary Kingsley, like the West African, was an animist who believed in living presences in Nature. In her narrative West African steamers are mad adventurers with a "mania for bush, and the delusion that they are required to climb trees" (*TWA*, 127); the cargo boat *Lagos* is portrayed as a slightly wanton lady "shamelessly whistling" and "squarking" for cargo as she sidles her way down the Coast. Similarly, mangrove trees become coquettes "displaying their ankles in a way that shocked Captain Lugard" (*TWA*, 88).

Parody of the style and content of other travel books about Africa also enlivens *Travels in West Africa* and warns readers not to expect a predictable narrative of dramatic encounters and heroic postures. On occasion, the narrator sets the stage for such a clichéd scene, only to reverse her reader's expectations by parodying the language and the histrionics of such episodes. For example, Kingsley, who held that it was "utter idiocy" to flourish a revolver and threaten to shoot in Africa (*TWA*, 330), took aim in the following passage at the conventional self-portrayal of the white hunter in Africa:

I know exactly how I ought to have behaved. I should have felt my favourite rifle fly to my shoulder, and then, carefully sighting for the finest specimen, have fired. The noble beast should have stumbled forward, recovered itself, and shedding its life blood behind it have crashed away into the forest. I should then have tracked it, and either with one well-directed shot have given it its quietus, or have got charged

by it, the elephant passing completely over my prostrate body; either
termination is good form, but I never have these things happen, and
never will. (*TWA*, 258)

She also poked fun at the myth of the "daring rescue." When
Kiva, one of her bearers, was about to be cooked and eaten by
a creditor because of his default on a debt, Kingsley drily observed: "I dare say I ought to have rushed at him and cut his
bonds, and killed people in a general way with a revolver, and
then flown with my band to the bush; only my band evidently
had no flying in them, . . . so I shouted Azuna to the Bankruptcy Court, and got a Fan who spoke trade English to come
and interpret for me" (*TWA*, 285). The pointlessness and stupidity of flying "light–heartedly" into the dangerous African
bush becomes evident in this passage when such ludicrous conduct
is proposed, scrutinized by the speaker's coolly rational mind,
and then rejected. A canny calculation of risks and a knowledge
of African psychology are clearly more germane to the situation
than schoolboy histrionics.

Obviously, Mary Kingsley had little use for those travellers
who use Africa primarily as an arena for testing their masculinity
or their British superiority. She mocks the behavior of big-game
hunters by first imagining all the deadly aquatic sports that one
might pursue in West Africa—such as slaying sharks with knives
or spearing sting rays—and then concludes that "there is quite
enough danger in either sport to satisfy a Sir Samuel Baker; for
myself, being a nervous, quiet, rational individual, a large cat-
fish in a small canoe supplies sufficient excitement" (*WAS*, 82).
The climactic placing of the key word "rational" tips the balance
of the sentence in favor of the sane behavior of such "nervous"
travellers. A master of understatement, Kingsley often parodies
fustian rhetoric; in her account of an escape from an armed party
of cannibals who were chasing her canoe, the voice of the reliable
scientist deflates the romantic, exaggerated prose of the adventure
story: "Regardless of danger, I grasped the helm, and sent our
gallant craft flying before the breeze down the bosom of the great
wild river (that's the proper way to put it, but in the interests
of science it may be translated into crawling towards the middle)"

(*TWA*, 343). In *Travels in West Africa* such comic deflation is also directed against the jargon of contemporary psychology, newspaper reporting, and religion.

When inflated rhetoric masks social and political attitudes that Kingsley regards as dangerous, however, she unleashes the full force of her satiric wit. For instance, she strongly disagrees with those who argue that Africans are innocent children, mystical dreamers, cruel savages, or "undeveloped" white men to be judged by European standards (*TWA*, 659); instead she contends that they are human beings who possess "a remarkable mental acuteness and a large share of common sense" (*TWA*, 439) and who have a distinctive and rich cultural heritage. She often uses humor to force her readers to acknowledge the legitimacy of African cultural institutions and to startle them out of complaisant assumptions of cultural superiority. Thus, she concludes her narrative of a tense encounter between Kiva and one of his creditors in a remote Fan village by drawing a startling cultural parallel. The creditor plans to collect his debt by seizing and eating Kiva, and Kingsley observes:

Evidently this was a trace of an early form of the Bankruptcy Court; the court which clears a man of his debt, being here represented by the knife and the cooking pot; the white-washing, as I believe it is termed with us, also shows, only it is not the debtor who is whitewashed, but the creditors doing themselves over with white clay to celebrate the removal of their enemy from his sphere of meretricious activity. This inversion may arise from the fact that whitewashing a . . . [person] who was about to be cooked would be unwise, as the stuff would boil off the bits and spoil the gravy. There is always some fragment of sound sense underlying African institutions. (*TWA*, 285)

With a masterful control of tone, Kingsley evokes not only laughter but some serious thought about comparative culture. On another occasion she makes explicit the parallels that are only implicit in this passage: the African is "a logical, practical man, with feelings that are a credit to him, and are particularly strong in the direction of property. . . . His make of mind is exceedingly like . . . [that] of thousands of Englishmen of the stand-no-nonsense, . . . house-is-his-castle type" (*WAS*, 318–19).

To Major Nathan Kingsley professes "a very lively hatred for those armchair fools who sit up here [in England] and play cat and banjo with Africa and call the performance 'civilizing the African and spreading Christianity.' "[65] Frequently, her satire is directed against such people and their assumptions. A discussion of the garment imposed on African women by missionaries, the Mother Hubbard, provides the occasion for a satiric comment on European attitudes:

Forgive me, [Kingsley writes] but I must break out on the subject of Hubbards; I will promise to keep clear of bad language let the effort cost me what it may. . . . I think these things are one of the factors producing the well-known torpidity of the mission-trained girl; and they should be suppressed in her interest, apart from their appearance, which is enough to constitute a hanging matter. . . . These garments are usually made at working parties in Europe; and what idea the pious ladies in England, Germany, Scotland, and France can have of the African figure I cannot think, but evidently part of their opinion is that it is very like a tub. . . . It is not in nature for people to be made to fit these things. So I suggested that a few stuffed negroes should be sent home for distribution in working-party centres, and then the ladies could try the things on. (*TWA*, 221)

The final Swiftean line cuts through to the central issue: European philanthropists regard the "native" not as a flesh-and-blood reality with a sophisticated culture but as a slightly dangerous curiosity to be transformed into something that will fit their conception of him. Unlike Mary Kingsley, these Europeans will confront the African only when he has been eviscerated and rendered as harmless as a stuffed animal trophy.

Kingsley's sophistication as a satirist of European attitudes can be gauged by comparing this passage to a similar discussion of Mother Hubbards in May French Sheldon's account of her African travels, *Sultan to Sultan*. Although, like Kingsley, Sheldon found these garments to be "preposterous," she couched her criticism of the advocates of such dresses in blandly diplomatic language: "Home societies were all the time sending out made-up articles of clothing, especially for the girls and women, that were totally

unsuitable for their position or the climate; and the good creatures, zealously devoted to the propagation of the gospel . . .
were constantly making requests that the converts in the mission
should be clothed with Christian decency."[66] In contrast, Kingsley directs satiric laughter against attitudes and behavior that
need reform. Alice Green, in a posthumous tribute to her friend
Mary Kingsley, analyzed her use of humor: Fired by "burning
desire to arrest the attention of a people comfortable and at
ease, . . . she would find a story, lighten it up with her humour,
and hope that even as they laughed they might unconsciously
catch the meaning shut up in the tale."[67]

Frequently, those comfortable people found their complacent
assumptions of cultural superiority being challenged. In her article, "The Development of Dodos," Kingsley had urged her
readers to "put yourself in his [the African's] place, and you'll
understand his attitude." In her books Kingsley uses comic reversals to force her readers to see things as an African would. For
example, after describing a scene in which she has helped a young
African catch a crab, Kingsley imagines the subsequent behavior
of that black woman: "Had there been a local newspaper, and
had she been on the staff and had a telegraph office handy, she
would doubtless have rushed away and telegraphed, 'Strange Case
of Intelligence in a White' " (WAS, 389). The civilized and the
uncivilized have changed places; the placid observer has become
the observed. In a similar use of about-face, Kingsley wrote that
she could hardly wait to "get back to the Coast and tell them
about my experiences in England."[68] Familiar, sedate Britain
becomes the exotic, unknown realm. Through these reversals,
Kingsley aimed to create a fresh climate of opinion in which new
verities could replace old prejudices.

Kingsley's humor also serves to undermine readers' prejudices
and to control their responses to horrifying or repulsive situations.
For example, she ironically describes the way in which Europeans
"inform" themselves about African matters: "Now polygamy is
. . . a difficult thing to form an opinion on, if . . . you go and
make a study of the facts. . . . It is therefore advisable to follow
the usual method employed by the majority of people. Just take

a prejudice of your own, and fix it up with the so-called opinions of people who go in for that sort of prejudice too" (*TWA,* 212). But she also used her wit more subtly to humor readers into suspending judgment about African practices likely to shock a Western sensibility and to evoke a hostile response. Her amusing account of Kiva before the African Bankruptcy Court is a case in point. So, too, is her discussion of cannibalism among the Fan tribe. Such cannibalism, she observes with carefully modulated understatement, presents no danger to white travellers but is "a bother" because the traveller must labor to keep her "black companions from getting eaten." Then her discussion shifts to adopt the African point of view: "The Fan is not a cannibal from sacrifical motives. . . . He does it in his common sense way. Man's flesh, he says, is good to eat, very good, and he wishes you would try it. Oh dear no, he never eats it himself, but the next door town does. . . . He does not buy slaves and fatten them up for his table as some of the Middle Congo tribes I know of do. He has no slaves, no prisoners of war, no cemeteries, so you must draw you own conclusions. No, my friend, I will not tell you any cannibal stories" (*TWA,* 330). So little is she disturbed by cannibalism that Kingsley finds the least Westernized Africans to be soul mates with whom she shares an essentially spiritual outlook on life.

Critics accused Kingsley of being flippant about cannibalism; but, as several of these passages make clear, she tries to present African practices in a way that will forestall any immediate, stereo-typical response from a European reader. The amusing re-creation of the cannibal's self-justifying voice in the above passage encourages the reader to listen sympathetically and to avoid a culturally conditioned response. Throughout her travel writing, Kingsley herself eschews sensationalism and cultivates a slightly amused objectivity about controversial topics like African polygamy, human sacrifice, the murder of twins, and trial by ordeal. For instance, when she finds "a human hand, three big toes, four eyes, two ears, and other portions of the human frame" in a bag hanging in a hut where she is spending the night, Kingsley calmly examines and then replaces these repugnant relics; speculates about their origin (they are "mementoes" of earlier meals); and comments wryly that, though it is "touching" that cannibals keep such remembrances, "it's an unpleasant practice when they hang the remains in the bedroom you occupy" (*TWA*, 273).

Clearly, the narrator of *Travels in West Africa* and of the later *West African Studies* uses humor as a political and educational tool, simultaneously demolishing misconceptions about, and shaping new attitudes toward, Africans. She also employs a kind of gallows humor, learned from her mentors, the veterans of many years on Africa's West Coast, to control her readers' responses to the death-filled land that she so appropriately called "La Belle Dame Sans Merci." On her first voyage to West Africa, the inexperienced young woman had been fascinated by the Old Coasters' stories of death and disease—stories in which the horrible subject matter was overlaid with humor. Kingsley found a powerful metaphor to describe this technique which she herself would mimic: it was like dusting over a rotting corpse "with jokes" so that 'it would hardly show at a distance" (*TWA*, 85). Hence, she describes the gigantic, disease-bearing insects of West Africa, first, by solemnly observing that 75 percent of them sting, "5 per cent bite, and the rest are either permanently or temporarily parasitic on the human race," and then by casting them as actors in a comic drama. "If you see a thing that looks like a cross between a flying lobster and the figure of Abraxas on a Gnostic gem," she warns with mock seriousness, "do not pay it the least attention" (*WAS*, 9). At Cabinda, she continues, "the insects used to come in round the hanging lamp at dinner time. . . . Ever and anon a big beetle with a terrible boom on would sweep in, go two or three times round the room and then flop into the soup plate, out of that, shake himself like a retriever and bang into some one's face, then flop on the floor" (*WAS*, 9). The exaggerated physical description of the insect, the amusing comparison to a dog, and the slapstick comedy which the bug enacts, all produce a laughter that wards off disgust.

Having learned from the Old Coasters that fear can be as deadly as the actual dangers of West Africa, Kingsley cultivated a humorous attitude which kept fear at bay. She warns any newcomer

to the Coast to "take the most cheerful view of these statements, . . . take every care short of getting frightened, which
is as deadly as taking no care at all" (*TWA*, 690). And she
portrays her own encounters with danger as if they are comic
interludes. With mock indignation she writes:

I hate holes, and especially do I hate these African ones, for I am
frequently falling, more or less, into them, and they will be my
end. . . . All . . . sorts I have tried, having pitched by day and night
into those, from three to twelve feet deep . . . and also into those from
twenty to thirty feet deep with pointed stakes at the bottom, artfully
disposed to impale the elephant. . . . But my worst fall was into a
disused Portugese well of unknown depth. . . . Just as I was convinced
that my fate was an inglorious and inverted case of Elijah . . . I was
being carried off, alive. (*TWA*, 582–83)

The matter-of-fact tone in which these accidents are cata-
logued, as well as the narrator's scientific interest in the precise
depth of the holes and the "artful" arrangement of the deadly
spikes, directs attention away from the suffering and danger.
Emotions like fear, pity, or anger are thus held at bay, her
personal courage minimized, and life-threatening situations de-
toxified. This conscious and persistent self-mockery found in
much of Kingsley's writing has both psychological and literary
causes. Obviously, it manifests a profound insecurity and a negative self-image; yet, clearly, it is also a literary mask assumed
to amuse the reader. Its effect is surprisingly complex. Logically,
such self-deprecation should engender a distrust in the authority
and reliability of the narrator, but in practice it wins the readers'
sympathy and liking for the entertaining—albeit inept and struggling—narrator.

In such passages the narrator herself is often the butt of the
ironic humor. Kingsley repeatedly depicted herself as an endearing clown—always in need of hairpins, plagued by an "intolerable
habit of getting into water," and transporting reeking "abomi-
nations full of ants"—her specimens (*TWA*, 6). Sometimes, she
is the hilariously inept traveller who, with the insouciance of a
Buster Keaton, falls through roofs, tumbles into game pits, or

steers her canoe into conservatories and the sides of hospitals (*TWA*, 426). In a number of theatrical scenes Kingsley plays a comic part. When a strong river current forces her and her crew to the shore only two hundred yards from a village, Kingsley creates a dramatic scene in which she is the star:

> I scrambled along [the bank], the men yelled and shouted and hauled the canoe, and the inhabitants of the village . . . came, legging it like lamp-lighters, after us, young and old, male and female, to say nothing of the dogs. Some good souls helped the men haul, while I did my best to amuse the others by diving headlong from a large rock on to which I had elaborately climbed, into a thick clump of willow-leaved shrubs. They applauded my performance vociferously, and then assisted my efforts to extricate myself, and during the rest of my scramble they kept close to me, with keen competition for the front row, in hopes that I would do something like it again. But I refused the encore, because, bashful as I am, I could not but feel that my last performance was carried out with all the superb reckless abandon of a Sarah Bernhardt, and a display of art of this order should satisfy any African village for a year at least. (*TWA*, 170–71)

The allusion to Sarah Bernhardt works on two narrative planes because Kingsley is both the unwitting entertainer of an African audience and the conscious clown of a tale designed to entertain her English readers.

The Conflicting Selves

Any discussion of the narrative technique of *Travels in West Africa* and *West African Studies* must acknowledge that these works have not one consistent narrator but rather a plurality of voices that group themselves around the sexual antipodes. The self-deprecating voice characterizes the persona of the lady traveller, the amusing spinster prone to "feminine nervousness" which makes her flee from wild animals: "I have seen at close quarters specimens of the most important big game of Central Africa, and, with the exception of snakes, I have run away from all of them" (*TWA*, 268). Such self-characterization, however, is inconsistent with Kingsley's behavior in Africa, where she stood calmly by the side of an African until the muzzle of his gun touched a gorilla's chest or where she liberated a leopard from a trap only to find it sniffing around her skirts instead of running away. How did this nervous, timid female respond? With a peremptory command, "Go home, you fool," which sent the leopard "flying."[69] Even the text of *Travels in West Africa* itself reveals that Miss Kingsley was no coward. One night she encountered a "whirling mass of animal matter," a dog and a leopard fighting within a yard of where she stood. "The leopard," she notes, "crouched, I think to spring on me. I can see its great, beautiful, lambent eyes still, and I seized an earthen water-cooler and flung it straight at them. . . . A noble shot, it burst on the leopard's head like a shell and the leopard went for bush one time" (*TWA,* 546). By slipping into trade English at the end, Kingsley lightens the tone of this dramatic encounter, but the essential reality of her courageous, effective action cannot be disguised. Rudyard Kipling praised her "utter fearlessness" and "that controlled power that seemed to give her natural command of all situations."[70]

Among the most striking inconsistencies in self-portraiture are the various sexual identities that Kingsley's narrator assumes. Sometimes the speaker portrays herself as a hardy, adventurous, confident, profane, masculine traveller—an Old Coaster who is proud of being a "sailorman" or a "Devil's man." Amused by claims that she can "swear like a trooper," this persona is a tough talker: "I would rather drink than fight with any of them" (*TWA,* 547). Even Macmillan seems to have been confused by her ventriloquism, for he commented that one of her stories seemed to be told by a man.[71] This speaker's actions match her aggressive speech: "We would each have killed the other if sufficient inducement were offered, and so we took a certain amount of care that the inducement should not arise" (*TWA,* 264). In this voice, the narrator can lecture the audience on the relative value of a gun and a knife to the traveller: "Always have your revolver ready loaded in good order, and have your hand on it when things are getting warm, and in addition have an exceedingly good bowie knife, not a hinge knife. . . . A knife is essential, because after wading neck deep in a swamp your revolver is neither use nor ornament until you have time to clean it" (*TWA,* 330).

This experienced, authoritative persona is always in control. When the African bearers try to subvert her ascent of Mungo by leaving behind the water supply so that she, like others before her, would be forced to retreat, Kingsley deals with their rebellion forcefully but not violently: "I express my opinion of them and of their [previous] victims in four words—send Monrovia boy . . . back to Buea . . . send cook with him as far as the camp . . . with orders to bring up three bottles of soda water I have left there, and to instruct the men there that as soon as the water arrives from Buea they are to bring it on up to the camp I mean to make at the top of the wall" (*TWA,* 574). The crisp imperatives of this journal entry, the decisive "I mean to make," and the tone of command compel the respect of both the Africans and the reader. Unlike H. M. Stanley, who was notorious for his use of whip and gun on his bearers, Kingsley managed to control her men through the force of her personality and her knowledge of psychology.

The persona that Kingsley creates in this passage differs in several intriguing ways from the voice she used to narrate the same experience in the article, "The Throne of Thunder," which appeared in *The National Review* (1896). Presented as a past-tense narrative rather than a first-person diary account, this version of Kingsley's ascent of Mungo Mah Lobeh projects a subtly different image of the "experiencing I." The narrator of the journal article responds to the news that the party is without water thus: "The suppression of this piece of information was evidently a trick of my men who thought that . . . I should return, and they should go safely home . . . but [I] saw that unless the affair was instantly tackled, it meant failure." In contrast, the speaker in *Travels* is a determined explorer who thinks *first* of the consequences to her venture—"this means failure unless tackled"—and only then of the reasons for the shortage—the intentional "trick" of the reluctant bearers. Moreover, this narrator is anxious to convince readers of her responsibility to her party and of her competence as a leader: "Had I known, of course, I would have brought up a sufficient supply." Unlike the sedate narrator of the journal article, this aggressive persona uses profanity (those mysterious four words), expresses anger openly, and manifests a rhetorical sophistication. The journal article ends rather anticlimactically: "the others said they would come on with the water, and sat down." The strong speaker of the book, however, "instructs" the men that "they are to bring" the water to the "camp I mean to make at the top of the wall." By concluding with her willed control over the men rather than their sedentary posture, Kingsley portrays herself in *Travels* as a self-confident leader.

Resembling this confident, authoritative voice is that of the serious scholar, which Kingsley often adopts to lecture readers on subjects that she knows thoroughly from both personal experience and profound study. This speaker asserts that "there is room for more white enterprise in the matter of river navigation [in West Africa]" (*TWA*, 634). She challenges the Colonial Office's policy of railroad development and confidently dismisses the opinions of trade "experts" as rooted in "fatal error" (*TWA*, 656). She even chides respected authorities like Dr. Nassau for not having "done more for science and geography": "Had he but had Livingstone's conscientious devotion to taking notes, . . . we should know far more than we do at present . . ." (*TWA*, 395).

But a counterbalancing voice identifies itself as both female and *ladylike*. This speaker defers to the "superior sex," reminds us that even in the jungle her attire is modest and appropriate to a London street, and confines herself to "woman's true sphere" when excitement or danger threatens (*TWA*, 193). This timid, proper persona eschews profanity and holds that "it is unladylike to go shooting things with a gun" (*TWA*, 545). The distinctions between this persona and her male counterpart correspond with Robin Lakoff's observations about the differences between female and male language use. Women, Lakoff contends, are conditioned to avoid strong, self-assertive means of expression (e.g., profanity or powerful adjectives) to express themselves in overly polite, ladylike phrases, and to trivialize their utterances, or to express themselves tentatively. The effect of such linguistic practices is to submerge a woman's personal identity.[72] The "masculine" speaker in *Travels in West Africa* imposes his will upon others; the "female," on the other hand, wishes that she could "flirt" with an official so she could get her way but ruefully admits that she doesn't know how. Thus she is doubly impotent, having neither male force nor feminine wile. The male persona is a reliable scholar, the female, flightly and illogical: "My brother would say, 'It's perfectly simple if you think about it;' but thinking is not my strong point" (*TWA*, 298). Occasionally, when she admits to any ability to think, Kingsley portrays herself as the farcical pedant whose disquisitions on pet subjects put even insomniacs to sleep (*WAS*, 191).

These conflicting voices express not only her complex, conflicting personal needs but also her sense of the putative expectations of the readers of these travel books. A reviewer in *Concord* labelled her "a very unwomanly woman" who uses "tainted language"[73] while the *Glasgow Herald* chided: "It is a pity that Miss Kingsley has not tried to write in a more ladylike manner."[74] Another reviewer commented on the sexual schizophrenia evident in her "perfectly original and distinctive style," which has "nothing about it that one is accustomed to associate with the word 'feminine.' " In fact, this commentator speculated that readers must have been astonished to learn that the author was "the prim and staid maiden lady that Miss Kingsley was."[75]

Twentieth-century readers can see what Kingsley's contemporaries could not: the assertive, competent male persona of the travel books reifies a fantasy self, the secure, confident public figure; the self-deprecating, demure female voice evinces the insecure, lonely, private self as well as the socially acceptable, public female self. The feminine voice reflects the Victorian sexual calculus to which Kingsley consciously ascribed: women have ordained social roles that demand a certain propriety and command a commensurate respect. When she perceives herself deviating from the expected role, Kingsley feels compelled to remind her reader that she is not challenging the fundamental distinction between male and female behavior. Therefore, in describing how she successfully shipped some ebony logs from the bank to a river steamer, Kingsley first must apologize for undertaking such a masculine task. Because the "superior sex" is "on its back with fever and sending its temperature up with worrying" about the logs, she agrees to handle the operation. As she directs the shipping from behind the woodpile, the captain of the steamer curses impatiently, unaware that he is dealing with a lady. Gleefully, Kingsley manages the man's job and then unmasks as a woman, embarrassing the profane captain: "When the thing went well, I did say things from behind the woodstack to the captain, [but] I did not feel justified in accepting his apologetic invitation to come on board and have a drink" (*TWA*, 651). Proud of being "one of the boys," Kingsley is also careful to maintain a ladylike reserve.

Although Kingsley admired many women—from beautiful African ladies, to selfless missionary wives, to her own Irish charwoman who "knocked some of the nonsense" out of a recalcitrant husband—she believed that women were inherently inferior to men. As Africans were an entirely different "species" from whites, so women were fundamentally different from and inferior to men: "I am certain," she averred, that "old Herodotus's division of the human race into feminine and masculine peoples has more in it than meets the eye. Take the white races. Your Hebrew and Teuton are masculine. . . . Take coloured races. . . . Your Negro and Melanesian are feminine."[76] In addition, "the mental difference between the two races is very similar to that between men and women among ourselves. A great woman, either mentally or physically, will excel an indifferent man, but no woman ever equals a really great man" (*TWA*, 659). As a woman, then, Kingsley feels akin to Africans, able to be their champion to the masculine British; however, as a woman she also believes herself to be inferior to a man like her brother. When Macmillan wrote urging Mary Kingsley to complete the biography of her father which her brother was supposed to have finished long before, she replied: "I am sorry about Charley but I have done my best . . . in waiting for him to come home before taking up the affair, but now if you like I will do it. You know I cannot do so well as he could. . . . (14 August 1899).[77]

Kingsley clearly sensed that femaleness was a liability to serious scientific work. Not only was her potential limited by the inherent inferiority of her sex, her work was exposed bo the prejudice of the male scientific establishment. To St. Loe Strachey she expressed regret that she was "only a woman" and thus her advocacy of the anthropological point of view in the public debates about Africa would carry less weight.[78] "If I were a man," she once wrote, "I'd have a love of a fight with the cabinet of comparative ethnologists."[79] By implication, a woman could neither join nor win such a fight. Paradoxically, Kingsley also believed that she had a special influence with the white traders—those "savage men"—because of her sex. In a sentence in which she portrays herself simultaneously as male and female, as Punch and Judy, she writes: "I make no pretence at being able to rule my Pappenheimers [the traders]—or more truly speaking my wife Judy—but they will listen to me, because I am a woman—more than they will to others. They will take abuse from me that coming from another would mean slaughter."[80] Although Kingsley compares herself to a "female patron saint of a band of brigands," she later slips into a characteristically self-mocking depiction of her influence: "I try to *lead* these men with a palm branch," she laments, but "two-thirds of my time I am rushing about . . . using the palm branch like a switch."[81] The saint is transformed into a scolding, harried farm wife; the image of female power yields to that of feminine impotence.

Clearly, Kingsley was confused about her sexual identity. Patricia Frazer Lamb even argues that she was "engaged in a complicated game of self-deception, to avoid being forced to resolve the paradox of the hero versus mock-hero, of demure lady versus adventurous woman."[82] Thus, when the *Athenaeum* praised Kingsley as "undoubtedly the first of her sex who had dared to face the manifold dangers of the pestilential regions of . . . barbarous Western Equatorial Africa"[83] and denigrated the other women in Africa—wives of officials and missionaries—for staying close to their comfortable homes, Kingsley angrily replied. In a letter to that journal she commends the noble self-sacrifices made by women who came to Africa out of "duty to their husbands" and claims that these women risk more by staying in one place than she did by travelling.[84] Kingsley goes on to celebrate the "equally creditable behavior under difficulties" of women at home in England. Yet this letter also alludes to "the morbid state of opinion regarding women's work" which makes it unpleasant "for any student who happens to be a woman to come before the public." Kingsley here seems to be both defending her own professional labors and also attacking those who would denigrate women's traditional labor in the home. Her statement is so ambiguous that it can be read either as a conservative reaction against the rhetoric of the "new woman" or as a defense of women's claim to respect in the male-dominated scientific world.

Kingsley strongly objected when the *Daily Telegraph* identified her as a champion of "the emancipation of her sex," and she expressed scorn for "those shrieking females and androgins" who were agitating for female suffrage.[85] In a lecture on 27 February 1900 before the Fawcett Society, a pro-suffrage group, she opposed giving women the vote because, she argued, they should shun the sordid world of politics (in which she herself was deeply immersed) and content themselves with being vocal, independent outsiders with no ties to party politics. Through the voting male members of their family they could in fact exert a powerful influence, she claimed, although she never explained how the disenfranchised could wield any effective power.[86] Perhaps because she felt that she had "failed miserably" in her attempts to shape the Colonial Office's African policy, Kingsley contended that women would not be good at politics anyway. She also insisted that women should not agitate for membership in scientific societies like the Royal Geographic Society because "if we women distinguish ourselves in Science in sufficiently large numbers at a sufficiently high level, the great scientific societies . . . will admit" us, or "we shall form . . . our own of equal eminence."[87] Yet she later observed that the presence of women could hinder scientific research in some societies because it would restrict the topics that could be publicly discussed in front of ladies. [88] Women, then, are both superior to and not good enough for political action, scientifically equal to, yet socially more restricted than, men.

A letter about suffrage to Matthew Nathan further illustrates her ambivalent attitude toward women: "I have been opposing women having the parliamentary vote this afternoon, and have had a grand time of it, and have been called an idealist and had poetry slung at me in chunks. Argument was impossible, so I offered to fight the secretary in the backyard, but she would not." [89] With a humorous twist, Kingsley slips into a male persona in the final clause, ironically adopting a pose that she parodied in her travel writing—the man who would sooner fight than talk or think. It is as though a masculine posture and tone of voice could exempt her from the emotionally taxing complexities of such a "female issue."

In her travel writings Kingsley occasionally adopts a similar, decidedly male voice to extricate herself verbally from situations in which femaleness is a liability. Through wit and verbal skill she manages to overcome the objections of officials to her travelling up the Ogowé without a husband. The page heading over the account of this victory identifies the protagonist as male: "A Wilful Man Has His Way." Likewise she silences an inquisitive boatman, who persists in asking for her husband, with abrupt and profane language which she demurely says is "unreportable" (*TWA*, 217). Kingsley once warned a female audience that a single woman in Africa must expect to be "perpetually embarrassed" by queries about her husband. Rather than admitting to her single state, the woman, Kingsley advised, should always say that she is "looking for" her husband in the direction that she wishes to travel anyway. Such a strategem elicits sympathy and help rather than "appalling questions." [90] Through this humorous but eminently practical advice, Kingsley reveals that when she is not masquerading as a male, she still feels in need of a disguise for her femaleness.

Writing to Macmillan, Kingsley also reveals her desire to disguise her gender by publishing her book either with no name on it or only with the initials "M.K." "I really cannot draw the trail of the petticoat over the Coast of all places," she observes, then adds, "neither can I have a picture of myself in trousers or another with excitement of that sort added. I went out there as a Naturalist, not as a sort of circus."[91] In refusing to cheapen her experiences to obtain popularity, Kingsley also implicitly acknowledges that to be identified as a female traveller is to risk a loss of credibility as a scientist. But the real cause of her anxiety about her name emerges in her subsequent remarks: "I have written it all with my eye on the 'Coast' who will of course know I was a lady and will also be the only people who will know the value of what I say." Present but unarticulated here is the fear that some readers might deny the value of her observations if they knew her sex, while others might conclude from the knowledge of her exploits and her sex that she is not "a lady." Only those who knew her on the Coast can reconcile those two sides of herself which even Kingsley finds to be incompatible. And she felt that any undue stress on her sex would render her "ridiculous and unladylike before them."

Thus, she was caught in an impossible position. To win acceptance for her ethnological and political ideas, Kingsley could never alienate her audience by letting them think that she was one of those radical "shrieking females": as a result, she had to affirm her allegiance to a restrictive code of female behavior that she herself did not always observe. Yet, ironically, this admission of femaleness possibly jeopardized her reputation as a scientist. Hence, she longed, as the above letter to Macmillan suggests, to obliterate her sexual identity altogether. The interplay of personal uncertainty about gender, a sense of political exigency, and a desire for scientific respectability produced a complex and sometimes baffling polyphony of narrative voices in Kingsley's writings. As she once confessed to Stephen Gwynn, "I am 'elusive.' I know it and it is malice aforethought."[92]

The Writings and Controversies 1897–1899

When *Travels in West Africa* was published early in 1897, the *Spectator* praised its "striking and original" approach to travel writing[93] while the *Athenaeum* asserted that "Miss Kingsley

. . . humorous and even comical as her method often is . . . must undoubtedly be taken seriously, for she displays keen powers of observation, far keener than those of most men who visit the coast."[94] Similarly, Dr. Günther, who had been responsible for Kingsley's decision to collect fish, enthusiastically lauded her "extraordinary gift of observation," her "indefatigable energy," and her "judicious selection of specimens."[95]

She returned with forty-three different species including an "absolutely new fish," which was named for her; a new snake; and a lizard that the British Museum had waited ten years to own.[96] Her literary endeavors were equally successful; "her public"—as she called Dr. Günther and the Liverpool trading firms—lauded her book. To Macmillan she wrote: "Liverpool telegraphed yesterday enthusiastically and today practically for six copies. I cannot resist sending you my greatest review, i.e. Günther."[97] The reading public at large found the book fascinating; sales were so good that a popular edition was projected (to be issued in 1900) and the royalties enabled Kingsley to plan a return to the Coast in January 1898. However, her brother's ever-changing plans, which delayed her departure, and the political controversies of 1897–1899, which engaged much of her intellectual and emotional energy, prevented Kingsley from embarking for West Africa. She was never to see the Coast again.

Frequently, during these exhausting, depressing, and politically complex years in which she found herself engaged in a "war," Kingsley longed for the freedom to "skylark" again in Africa. But the "party" with which she had allied herself on West African affairs, the Liverpool merchants like George Goldie and Alfred Jones, "nagged" her, so she claimed, to interest the public in West Africa through articles and lectures "with magic lantern slides."[98] A popular, witty speaker, Kingsley drew large crowds; in July 1897 she lectured to 1,700 people from "a red-velvet lined pulpit" at Highbury. Two years later she wrote a febrile letter to the trader John Holt describing a week in which she spoke to thousands at York, Newcastle, Edinburgh, Glasgow, Hawick, Birmingham, Halifax, and Birmingham again.[99] In addition, she continued to write about African attitudes toward property in "The Law and Nature of Property among the Peoples of the True Negro Stock" and toward spirits in "The Forms of Apparitions in West Africa." And in an article in *Fortnightly Review* (April 1898) she defended the interests of the traders by attacking popular misconceptions about "The Liquor Traffic with West Africa."

Mary Kingsley also began work on another book which was to contain ethnological material that had either been "crowded out" of *Travels* or had required "further investigation and comparison" (*WAS*, ix). This volume would include chapters excised from her first book—particularly the vibrant description of life on a West Coast steamer—and material from her lectures and published articles. Finally, this new book was to present "the most difficult thing I have ever had to do" (*WAS*, ix), a critique of the Crown Colony system of governing West Africa and a proposal for a restructuring of the imperial government. Composing this book, particularly its political sections, taxed Kingsley's organizational powers and rhetorical skills. Without the framework of the journey to lend a structure to her eclectic observations, she feared that her writing would become diffuse and incoherent.

West African Studies, as its title indicates, is not a travel book; instead, it is a 633-page assemblage of personal narrative, scholarship, and polemics about West Africa. It includes extensive appendices on an early voyage to the Oil Rivers (written by John Harford), on the natives of the Niger Coast Protectorate (written by Count de Cardi), and on trade goods used in seventeenth-century West Africa (written by Kingsley herself). With the exception of the two opening chapters, which were originally written for the travel book, this work is less poetic and less ebullient than its predecessor. The extensive discussions of Fetish (five chapters); of Imperialism, Trade, and Commerce in West Africa (two chapters); and of African notions of Property, Law, and Religion reveal Kingsley's "mania" for facts. In this work, scholarly intent holds in check the humor and the self-dramatization that had enlivened *Travels in West Africa*. The witty, self-mocking persona of that book is not absent in this more weighty volume, but she is definitely not on center stage. *Travels in West Africa* charms and convinces the reader because of the personality of its narrator; *West African Studies,* on the other hand, relies more heavily on facts and arguments.

But these arguments, spawned by contemporary political controversies, sorely taxed Kingsley's stylistic powers. Secure about her empirical knowledge but not about her forensic skill, she complained that "this new book, though it will seem flippant enough . . . is heavy work for me. I am holding onto the main idea . . . by the scruff of its neck, but the selection of facts that will bring that idea clearly out to the minds of people who do not know it is hard work."[100]

This "main idea" was that Britain should abolish the Crown Colony system of governing West Africa (through a Governor and Executive and Legislative Councils appointed by and responsible to the Colonial Office in London), replacing it with a council of merchants who would rule indirectly through the existing social organization of the African clans. For a direct, centralized bureaucratic governmental structure dominated by officials in London, Kingsley wanted to substitute a looser, indirect system of government dominated by the trading firms in Liverpool. Such a proposal indicates, in the opinion of John Flint, a "fanatical and unbalanced" devotion to the cause of the white traders.[101]

This advocacy of governmental reform in West Africa brought her into direct conflict with the Colonial Secretary, Joseph Chamberlain. Prior to Chamberlain's appointment, which took place in 1895 while Kingsley was making her first trip to the Coast, policymakers for Africa had been content to let merchants initiate and finance territorial development. Chamberlain, however, believed that the government should be directly involved in colonial development. In 1895 he affirmed that the African colonies should be regarded as "undeveloped estates . . . which can never be developed without Imperial assistance."[102] Such "assistance" in West Africa was to take the form of "scientific administration" of the colonies, pacification of the interior, official supervision of local chiefs, abolition of the slave trade, opening of railroads, and attraction of European investment capital. Chamberlain's imperial goals necessitated that Britain secure as yet unclaimed areas of West Africa from the French government, which was amassing substantial territory in the region. Thus, in 1897 he organized the West African Frontier Force under the direction of Frederick Lugard, who later became the first governor of the British protectorate and colony of Nigeria. Ordered to occupy as much land as he could without precipitating an armed confrontation with the French, Lugard proceeded into the interior, where he claimed lands for Britain by making treaties with local chiefs (some of whom had already made treaties with the French). After several encounters in 1898 between Lugard's force and the French, war seemed imminent; however, the disputes were settled diplomatically in July 1898 by the Niger Convention, which awarded France sizeable territory in West Africa and access to navigable sections of the Niger River in exchange for French acknowledgment of British hegemony on the Nile. In an article on "The Transfer of the Niger Territories," Kingsley confesses that her "sporting instinct" makes her admire France's bold imperial scheme: "I do not grudge France one mile of her African Empire nor its glorious future."[103]

Kingsley did "grudge," however, Chamberlain's treatment of the great merchant adventurer Sir George Goldie. Because the Royal Niger Company had been a bone of contention between France and England and because, as a private company, it was ill equipped to compete militarily with the French expeditions along the Upper Niger, Chamberlain wanted to expropriate it "lock, stock and barrel"[104] and did so in 1898. To Chamberlain, Goldie's company was a liability because it did not fit into his imperial plan for West Africa; to Mary Kingsley, the R.N.C. epitomized all that was good about the "old way" of administering West Africa. Like Kingsley, Goldie believed in indirect rule. "Even an imperfect and tyrannical native administration, if its extreme excesses were controlled by European supervision," he argued, would be preferable to the "well-intentioned but ill-directed efforts of European magistrates." He contended that "the welfare of the native races" would be best served by "the general policy of ruling on African principles through native rulers."[105]

As a crusader for "the introduction of anthropology into statecraft" and for a sympathetic and respectful attitude toward African institutions, Kingsley saw Goldie as an ally, whose defeat signaled doom for her own campaign. Furthermore, the demise of the R.N.C. indicated a waning of the trader's influence in Africa and a waxing of the civil servant's. Kingsley saw evidence of the dangerous consequences of allowing Africa to be ruled by bureaucrats, rather than by students of African culture, in the controversy over the imposition of a hut tax in Sierra Leone in 1898.

Sierra Leone had been declared a protectorate in 1896 and, in accordance with Chamberlain's ideas of "scientific" administration, plans were drawn up for a railroad, slavery was prohibited, and a tax of 5s. per hut was levied to support the increased governmental activity. The Africans, however, opposed the tax; a group of chiefs met to protest its imposition; some refused to pay and were treated disrespectfully or brutally; violence flared against missionaries and Europeanized natives. As an anthropologist, Kingsley understood one of the causes for the rebellion; in an article called "The Position of Britain in the World" in the *Spectator*, [106] she explained that "this form of taxation is abhorrent to the principles of African law" because in that legal system "the thing you pay anyone a regular fee for is a thing that is not your own." To an African, she continued, British actions appeared anomalous: first Britain prohibited chiefs from engaging in the lucrative slave trade, then challenged their right to own slaves, then imposed a police force to implement these unpopular laws, and finally financed this force by taxing African property.

Kingsley's public attack on the hut tax was cited in Parliament by the Irish Nationalist Michael Davitt (who, of course, was looking for other instances of British colonial injustice). A commission of inquiry under Sir David Chalmers began an investigation; Kingsley continued her campaign in a series of lectures and in four articles in the *Morning Post;* and Joseph Chamberlain turned to Kingsley for advice. To her friend John Holt, Kingsley wrote amusingly: "Chamberlain is manifesting a desire to be taught. He is horribly frightened of being known to communicate with me, à la Saul and the witch of Endor. . . . I secretly inserted into him on a dozen sides the horror of the thing he has done with his hut tax. . . ."[107] The role of knowledgeable but disreputable outsider seems to suit her here as the pose of a rakish adventurer fits her travel writings. In weekly correspondence with Chamberlain she repeatedly condemned the present government of West Africa which "necessitates interfering with native races" and insisted that "to make West Africa succeed-pay-advance, the system of dealing with it must be remodelled. . . ."[108]

To the remodelling of that system Kingsley turned her attention in 1898, devoting almost one hundred pages of *West African Studies* to the delineation of a plan for ruling West Africa through an African Council composed of representatives of the major trading firms, who would be empowered to vote supplies and appoint a Governor-General. The administrative structure that Kingsley imagined would consist of two sub-councils (one composed of British lawyers and doctors, one of native chiefs), various district commissioners and sub-commissioners in Africa, and, of course, her beloved traders, who would be the agents of local government. Consistent with her fundamental priorities, this plan maximized freedom for the trader, utilized existing African social structures, and minimized the government's interference with African life. Kingsley's specific plan was never adopted; but, by the early twentieth century, Britain was ruling Nigeria indirectly through African cultural institutions. The woman who had fought with her "back against the wall . . . for the employment of anthropological knowledge in the government of tropical Africa" and who combated the misconception that "any concession to native ideas shows weakness and involves a loss of prestige"[109] had partially won her battle. Bernard Porter has observed that Kingsley "forged that alliance between Liverpool trade and colonial reform which . . . provide[d] one of the main strands in the discussion of African policy after her death."[110]

But a sense of personal inadequacy haunted Kingsley, the public champion: "I feel I damage a good cause by my vain attempts to give an absolutely fair picture of the thing as it is. . . . I do

work so hard to be fair and clear and I so very rarely succeed in
making myself either."[111] In her utterances of 1898–1899 self-
lacerating doubt and insecurity alternate with the self-right-
eousness of a person who martyrs herself for a cause: "I am very
lonely and worried in this African affair and I care about it
bitterly."[112] In a piece in *The Pall Mall Gazette* (28 July 1899)
she portrayed herself as "used to finding myself rather lonely
when a fight is on and well provided with companions when it
comes to a triumphal procession." To E. D. Morel, she lamented:
"I felt so lonely having been . . . regarded as almost blasphemous
for saying anything against English imperial government."[113]
Ten days later, she told Morel of her anger and frustration: "I
feel so savage about my own short comings. . . . Forgive a
fractious letter [but] I am very cross with things up here—with
this Jubilee swelled-head Imperialism that is conceited beyond
words" (20 February 1899).

These years of political struggle were also years of personal trial
and physical exhaustion for Mary Kingsley. Never a physically
hardy person despite her intrepid physical accomplishments,
Kingsley so weakened herself by her writing and lecturing sched-
ule that in January 1898 she developed a bad case of influenza
which eventually led to a bout with typhoid fever. And, in March
of that year, Kingsley's friend, the former governess who had
married George Goldie and who "loved" Kingsley herself,[114]
died. "Shattered" by the loss of Lady Goldie, who "fascinated"
and "exercised an immense influence" over her,[115] and exhausted
by the strains of moving into a new house on the Hammersmith
Road, Kingsley confessed that she was feeling "like an uninsured
wreck."[116]

Intellectually active despite her anxieties, Kingsley produced
two books in these years: a short narrative history of West Africa
written for H. Marshall's Empire Series and a volume of her
father's writings. Several years before, Mary's brother had agreed
to write a memoir of his father for Macmillan. When it eventually
became clear that he would never complete the work, his sister
reluctantly assumed the editorship of the volume that became
Notes on Sport and Travel, a compilation of George Kingsley's

travel writings prefaced by a lively biography of three generations of the Kingsley family. Writing *The Story of West Africa* proved to be another labor of love, for it enabled her to reread the early navigators and pirates whose works she had admired since childhood; moreover, it gave her an opportunity to reiterate her views on the integral relationship between British imperialism and mercantilism: "That England at home has not cared [for West Africa] you see written across the page of this history . . . what Empire we have down there has been forced on home authorities by the energy of the far-seeing merchants—not fostered by the Government."[117] She also included a panegyric to the African peoples whose culture she had studied for the past five years: "These negroes are a great world race—a race not passing off the stage of human affairs, but one that has an immense amount of history before it. Whatever we do in Africa today, a thousand years hence, there will be Africans to thrive and suffer from it" (*Story*, 19).

In the century's final year Kingsley's emotional resources were strained not only by her writings and by her campaign to repeal the hut tax and to disseminate anthropological knowledge but also by her developing relationship with Major Matthew Nathan. Nathan, a member of the Royal Engineers and the Secretary of the Colonial Defense Committee, had been appointed as interim governor of Sierra Leone while Governor Frederick Cardew returned to London to justify his behavior in the hut tax crisis. Soon after their meeting in February 1899, Mary Kingsley was writing Nathan febrile letters in which political and anthropological self-justification, self-denigratory revelations, and veiled pleas for sympathy tumbled over each other. "As a general rule," Mary wrote, "it is a matter of simply no importance whether anyone, from Joe Chamberlain to the dustman, understands me or no, but you are the exception." Then, pessimistically she added: "I suppose, with the irony of fate, you don't care a row of pins about understanding me."[118] To Stephen Gwynn, she gushed like an adolescent in the throes of her first romance: "I dote on the military and have a weakness for the Nation-Israel;"[119] to John Holt, she called Nathan "a valued friend of mine" and joked about her family's perplexity over her attraction to Jewish men. [120] In a letter to Nathan himself she first prophesies that "you won't understand me," then exclaims that "if I were a king in Babylon and you were a Christian slave . . . I should not have the power to willingly or wittingly mislay your matchbox," and finally pleads "remember as kindly as you can that melancholy thing that will always serve you and fear you."[121]

Whether this woman, who claimed "I know nothing myself of love,"[122] was indeed enamored of Nathan is problematic. Certainly she strained to convince Nathan of her trustworthiness as a commentator on Africa and, therefore, of the justice of her opposition to the hut tax, and she protested too much to Gwynn that a tête-à-tête between Nathan and her should not be interpreted in "some wild romantic form."[123] It is to Nathan that she boasts: "I have what no other white has just now—the entire confidence of the educated nig throughout West Africa"[124] (27 January 1900). Feeling herself to have "muddled" her political fights and to have been "beaten on that West African thing,"[125] she seems to have tried to justify herself by private appeals to Nathan that were calculated to win human sympathy for her public labors—and perhaps for her personal life as well. But even her wooing of Nathan has political overtones since he was a man possessed of political power and influence in West Africa. When she teases him about "fascinating my Chambers of Commerce— just when I was making up my mind that I was safely in possession of their affections"[126] she betrays her anxiety that someone other than she, someone with different political views, might become the spokesman for her beloved traders. Therefore, her desire to ingratiate herself with Nathan may also be the desire to win a political ally rather than a rival. Since his good opinion of her as a person and as a scholar mattered greatly to Kingsley, she was deeply "grieved" by their disagreements. With a chagrin that is only partly masked by the humorous distance she adopted, Kingsley wrote to Stephen Gwynn in February 1900 of the "most distressing row" she had had with Nathan.[127] Unfortunately, Kingsley was right about the ironies of fate, for this man apparently never embraced Kingsley's point of view and is reported by her friends to have deprecated her after her death. [128]

Although Kingsley was still passionately concerned with West Africa as the Victorian era drew to a close, her nation's attention was focused on South Africa, where the British and the Afrikaners were again in conflict. In March 1900 Kingsley decided, as she had almost eight years earlier when the domestic framework of her life collapsed, to journey to Africa. This time, however, her destination was South Africa, where she was ostensibly going to collect fish from the Orange River for the British Museum. However, it is clear that, feeling herself to be a political failure, Kingsley was in fact returning to the activity at which she knew she was adept—nursing. All of her adult life Kingsley felt that her "home" was "in the valley of the shadow of death." "I must reconcile myself to it, build my Shimbec there and settle down," she wrote to Sir Arthur Lyall in May 1898. Fatalistically, she told a friend: "I am going to South Africa nursing and I may not return."[129]

Indeed, as soon as she arrived, Kingsley volunteered for nursing duties and was assigned to the hospital for Boer prisoners of war at Simonstown. A letter to her friend, the author Alice Green, which exposes the horrible conditions at the hospital where patients were dying at an alarming rate from enteric fever, also reveals some of Kingsley's private reasons for returning to the familiar world of the sick room:

I am down in the ruck of life again. Whether I shall come up out of this, . . . I don't know. It is a desperate game I am playing here, and it is doubtful. One nurse and an orderly who have only been on two days are down themselves. But if I do not, . . . dear lady, I am eternally grateful to you for all your tenderness . . . for me. I who was and am and never shall be anything but a muddler. All this work here, the stench, the washing, the enemas, the bed pans, the blood, is my world. Not London society, politics, that gateway into which I so strangely wandered—into which I don't care a hairpin if I never wander again. . . . Remember it is this *Haute Politique* that makes me have to catch large powerful family men by the tails of their night-shirts at midnight, stand over them when they are sinking, tie up their jaws when they are dead. Five and six jaws a night have I had of late to tie up. DAMN the *Haute Politique.* [130]

But, despite the disclaimers in this letter, Kingsley had not withdrawn entirely from the public political sphere. On the voyage to South Africa she wrote to St. Loe Strachey in March 1900, urging him to meet with the Liverpool trader, A. L. Jones, to discuss the "service rendered to the State by the mercantile marine." [131] She also addressed a long letter to the editor of *The New African,* urging him to continue her work by educating the public about African culture and fighting for African nationalism. With hard-nosed political candor, Kingsley wrote to Strachey in May 1900 about the Anglo-Boer War: "It seems to me absolute rot for people like our Conciliation Committee to think any good can be done by half measures. You have got to choose whether you will have free Englishmen here or free Boers. I say we must have free Englishmen because of the Imperio-geographical position of the place, but I am perfectly certain that that means enslaving the Boers. Your freedom of institutions, etc.,etc.,etc., is slavery to them. . . ." [132] Finally, just as she had presented the facts of West Africa, as she had observed them, to the British public, so she felt obliged to document the conditions in the hospital and the conduct of the authorities because of the "awful row" over the war that was sure to erupt in the House of Commons. In a letter to Mrs. Green, published in the *Times* (8 August 1900), Kingsley detailed the filth, the smells, and the nightmarish illnesses of the prisoners. She also criticized the lack of planning and scientific knowledge of the British authorities. Clearly, even though she had ostensibly abandoned politics, Kingsley still had a clear conviction of her responsibility as an educator of the public.

However, the voice that had entered into so many "rows" in the last five years of the nineteenth century was soon to be silenced. Exhausted by years of grueling work and personal disappointment, and frantically battling appalling conditions in order to transform "chaos into order," a "mortuary into a sanatorium," [133] Kingsley herself contracted enteric fever and died on 3 June 1900. She had been in South Africa only two months.

In accordance with her dying wishes, this woman with the buccaneering spirit was buried at sea off the Cape of Good Hope. According to her fellow workers at the hospital, Kingsley had been "the one bright spot for us, always with some amusing tale when we were at our lowest ebb."[134] Dr. Carré, the chief medical officer of the hospital, who had worked by her side, saluted Kingsley as "a thoroughly good woman of giant intellect."[135]

The tributes that poured in after her death universally stressed both her humanity—evident in her compassion and capacity for friendship—and her scholarly achievement. Captain R. S. Rattray, a scholar of the Ashanti tribe of West Africa, called Kingsley "the greatest white woman who ever went to West Africa" and added that "in some ways I think she was inspired."[136] Lord Cromer affirmed that "he had never met a woman who impressed him so much as having the mind of a statesman."[137] George Goldie hailed her for having "the brain of a man and heart of a woman."[138] The *Spectator* observed in her obituary that Kingsley possessed "an intellect which . . . was of the first class and . . . a wealth of adventurous experience which belongs to few men, and to no other woman, of this generation."[139]

Ironically, these tributes are predicated on the very sexual dichotomies that so bounded Kingsley's definition of her self and her capabilities. Unable to be a statesman, or sailorman, or literary man, she nonetheless became a scholar, a traveller, a polemist, and an author. Convinced of her own insignificance and of the fact that "the best part of me is all this doubt and self-distrust and melancholy and heartache over other people,"[140] she became in fact an important political figure in the late nineteenth-century debate about Africa. John Flint even considers her "a brilliant theorist"[141] who "revolutionize[d]" the attitude toward Africa of British officials and the informed public.[142] But the personal cost of her successes was high: "I put an armour and corruscating wit . . . when I go out to battle. If I did not— well, I should be . . . hurt and embittered and . . . unfit for combat."[143]

Chapter Five

Conclusion

The Achievement

The achievement of women as travellers to Africa cannot be measured in terms of new territory explored, for, with the exception of Mary Kingsley, they did not generally venture into uncharted lands. Neither can their accomplishments as travel writers be assessed in terms of their elaboration of the predominantly male myth of Africa in nineteenth-century British consciousness. As Susan Greenstein observes, "the experience of women in Africa cannot be adequately transcribed in the adventurer's vocabulary of the central tradition."[1] In that tradition, the heroic masculine explorer confronts a dangerous continent—often perceived as feminine—which must be dominated by the force of his will. Women travellers, in contrast, develop strategies of accommodation, not confrontation or domination, and write richly eclectic, loosely structured narratives of their discoveries about the continent, its peoples, and their own psyches. Women like Katharine Petherick, Louisa Hutchinson, M. A. Pringle, Lucie Duff Gordon, Florence Dixie, and Mary Kingsley, in fact, discover a special sympathy for the strange and sometimes hostile peoples among whom they travel. Using their own experiences, these travellers often try to debunk popular stereotypes about Africans, "emphasizing an 'anthropological' authenticity of detail."[2] Indeed, anthropology was one of the professions in which nineteenth-century women first distinguished themselves.

The male African traveller emerges from his own narrative or from the "novels of empire" as a heroic figure; the female traveller, however, is often calculatedly unheroic. Either by adapting the male models or by skirting the male tradition altogether, British women travellers to Africa search for modes of presenting themselves and their experiences that accommodate both their own sense of self and their society's expectations about women. Understating their valor and their suffering, the personae of these travel books sometimes use humor to minimize the physical dangers they endure. Occasionally, they describe a valor different from that epitomized by male travellers; this heroism, rooted in fortitude and patience, achieves its triumphs through adaptation, not conquest. Strong yet self-deprecating, unselfconsciously courageous yet acutely conscious of the impressions they make on others, the personae of these writings are often complex characters. And, in some instances, their complexity is intensified by journeys that are not only physical ordeals but psychological rites of passage.

Thus, the Victorian British women who travelled to and wrote about Africa in the nineteenth century seem to define an alternate tradition, different both in content and form from that of their male counterparts. Their odysseys, though of widely varying literary sophistication, are of enduring interest because they detail encounters with new worlds that sometimes open new possibilities for the female self.

Notes and References

Preface

1. F. A. Kirkpatrick, "The Art of Travel 1700–1900," *Cambridge History of English Literature,* vol. 14, part 3, *The Nineteenth Century* (New York: Macmillan Co., 1939), p. 265.

Chapter One

1. Lady Anne Brassey, *A Voyage in the "Sunbeam"* (London: Longmans, Green, 1878); Constance Gordon-Cummings, *At Home in Fiji* (London and Edinburgh: W. Blackwood and Sons, 1881), and *A Lady's Cruise on a French Man of War* (London and Edinburgh: W. Blackwood and Sons, 1882); Lady Anne Blunt, *A Pilgrimage to Nejd* (1881; rpt. London: Frank Cass, 1968); Amelia Edwards, *A Thousand Miles Up the Nile* (London: Longmans, Green, 1877); Lucie Duff Gordon, *Letters from Egypt* (1862–1869) (London: Routledge and Kegan Paul, 1969); Fanny Trollope, *Domestic Manners of the Americans* (London: Whittaker, Treacher and Co., 1832); Harriet Martineau, *Society in America* (London: Saunders and Otley, 1837); Isabella Bird Bishop, *Unbeaten Tracks in Japan,* 2 vols. (London: John Murray, 1880), *Korea and Her Neighbours,* 2 vols. (London: John Murray, 1898), and *The Yangtze Valley and Beyond* (London: John Murray, 1899); Annie Taylor's diary was printed in William Carey, *Travel and Adventure in Tibet* (London: Hodder and Stoughton, 1902).

2. Lilias Campbell Davidson, *Hints to Lady Travellers At Home and Abroad* (London: Iliffe and Son, 1889), p. 1, and Elizabeth Bisland, "The Art of Travel," *The Woman's Book* (New York: Charles Scribner's, 1894), p. 373.

3. Dorothy Middleton, *Victorian Lady Travellers* (London: Routledge and Kegan Paul, 1965), p. 4.

4. Ellen Moers, *Literary Women* (New York: Doubleday and Co., 1976), points to the pervasive imagery of caged birds in writing by women.

5. W. H. Davenport Adams, *Celebrated Women Travellers of the Nineteenth Century* (London: W. Swan Sonnenschein, 1883), p. 2.

6. Davidson, *Hints to Lady Travellers,* p. 154.

7. Paul Fussell, *Abroad: British Literary Traveling Between the Wars* (New York: Oxford University Press, 1980), p. 203.

8. *Girls' Own Annual,* 16 January 1886, p. 252.

9. Davidson, *Hints to Lady Travellers,* p. 154.

10. Bisland, "The Art of Travel," p. 373.

11. Davidson, *Hints to Lady Travellers,* pp. 11–12.

12. May French Sheldon, *Sultan to Sultan* (Boston: Arena Publishing, 1892), p. 136.

13. Susan Greenstein, "Sarah Lee, the Woman Traveller, and the Literature of Empire," *Design and Intent in African Literature,* ed. David Dorsey, Stephen Arnold, and Phanuel Egejuru (Washington, D.C.: Three Continents Press, 1981), and Patricia Frazer Lamb, "The Life and Writings of Mary Kingsley: Mirrors of the Self " (Ph.D. diss., Cornell University, 1977), both have valuable discussions of these points.

14. Mary Wollstonecraft, *A Vindication of the Rights of Woman* (1792; rpt. New York: W. W. Norton and Co., 1975), p. 60.

15. Margery Perham and J. Simmons, *African Discovery: An Anthology of Exploration* (1942; rpt. Evanston, Ill.: Northeastern University Press, 1970), p. 4. Katherine Frank, "Voyages Out: Nineteenth-Century Women Travelers in Africa" (Paper delivered at the Women's Public Lives Institute, University of Kansas, January 1981), argues persuasively for a sexual interpretation of the male "penetration" of Africa.

16. Fussell, *Abroad,* p. 39.

17. F. A. Kirkpatrick, "The Art of Travel 1700–1900," *Cambridge History of English Literature,* p. 283.

18. John Tallmadge, "From Chronicle to Quest: The Shaping of Darwin's 'Voyage of the Beagle,' " *Victorian Studies* 23 (Spring 1980): 328.

19. Fussell, *Abroad,* p. 207.

20. Kirkpatrick, "The Art of Travel," p. 272.

21. Charles Batten, *Pleasurable Instruction: Form and Convention in Eighteenth Century Travel Literature* (Berkeley: University of California Press, 1978), p. 81.

22. Alexander von Humboldt, *Personal Narrative of Travels to the Equinoctial Regions of America,* trans. Thomasina Ross (London: H. G. Bohn, 1852), p. 105.

23. Norman Douglas, *Experiments* (New York: Robert McBride and Co., 1925), pp. 8–9.

24. Elenore Smith Bowen [Laura Bohannan], *Return to Laughter: An Anthropological Novel* (1954; rpt, Garden City, N.Y.: Anchor-Doubleday, 1964), p. xiv.

25. Batten, *Pleasurable Instruction,* p. 44.

26. Tallmadge, "From Chronicle to Quest," pp. 329–30.

27. Ibid., p. 326.

28. T. D. MacLulich, "Canadian Exploration as Literature," *Canadian Literature* 81 (Summer 1979): 75.

29. Samuel White Baker, *The Albert N'yanza Great Basin of the Nile,* 2 vols. (London: Macmillan and Co., 1866), 1:viii.

30. Henry Morton Stanley, *Through the Dark Continent,* 2 vols. (London: Sampson, Low, Marston, Searle, and Rivington, 1878), 1:1–2.

31. Mary H. Kingsley, *Travels in West Africa* (1897; 3rd. ed. rev. London, 1965), p. i.

32. Wollstonecraft, *A Vindication,* p. 60.

33. Mitzi Meyers, "Mary Wollstonecraft's Letters Written . . . in Sweden: Toward Romantic Autobiography," *Studies in the Eighteenth Century,* vol. 8, ed. Roseann Runte (Madison: University of Wisconsin Press, 1979), p. 166.

34. Suzanne Juhasz, " 'Some Deep Old Desk or Capacious Hold-All': Form and Women's Autobiography," *College English* 39 (February 1978): 663–68.

35. Dorothy Hammond and Alta Jablow, *The Myth of Africa* (New York: Library of Social Sciences, 1977), pp. 62–63.

36. James Casada, "Literature and Exploration," *The Discoverers: An Encyclopedia of Explorers and Exploration,* ed. Helen Delpar (New York: McGraw-Hill, 1980), p. 16.

37. Baker, *The Albert N'yanza,* 1:287–91.

38. Winwood Reade, *African Sketchbooks* (London: Smith Elder, 1873), 1:52.

39. Hammond and Jablow, *The Myth of Africa,* pp. 96–97.

Chapter Two

1. Phebe Hanaford, *Women of the Century* (Boston: B. B. Russell, 1877), p. 632.

2. *Times* (London), 14 November 1865.

3. Anne Baker, ed., *Morning Star: Florence Baker's diary of the expedition to put down the slave trade on the Nile, 1870–73* (London: William Kimber, 1972).

4. Mr. and Mrs. Petherick, *Travels in Central Africa and Explorations of the Western Nile Tributaries,* 2 vols. (London: William Kimber, 1872), 2:632.

5. A Lady [Elizabeth Melville], *A Residence at Sierra Leone,* ed. Caroline Norton (London, 1849; rpt. London: Frank Cass and Co., 1968). All textual references are from the 1968 edition.

6. Harriet Ward, *Five Years in Kaffirland,* 2 vols. (London, 1848).

7. John Mack Faragher, *Women and Men on the Overland Trail* (New Haven: Yale University Press, 1979), p. 142.

8. Lady M. A. Barker (Broome), *A Year's Housekeeping in South Africa* (London, 1877).

9. Julie Roy Jeffrey, *Frontier Women: The Trans-Mississippi West 1840–1880* (New York: Hill and Wang, 1979), pp. 1–21.

10. Adams, *Celebrated Women Travellers,* p. 456.

11. Monica Wilson and Leonard Thompson, eds., *The Oxford History of South Africa,* vol. 2, *South Africa 1870–1966* (Oxford: Clarendon Press, 1971), p. 263.

12. Louisa Hutchinson, *In Tents in the Transvaal* (London, 1879).

13. Philip Curtin, *The Image of Africa: British Ideas and Actions, 1750–1850* (Madison: University of Wisconsin Press, 1964), p. 324.

14. David Livingstone, *Missionary Travels and Researches in South Africa* (London: Ward, Lock, and Co., 1857), p. 102.

15. M. A. Pringle, *Towards the Mountains of the Moon: A Journey in East Africa* (London, 1884).

16. Annie B. Hore, *To Lake Tanganyika in a Bath Chair* (London, 1886).

17. Annie B. Hore to Foreign Secretary, London Missionary Society, August 1887, Archives of the Council for World Mission, London University, School of Oriental and African Studies.

18. Hore to Secretary, Archives of the Council for World Mission.

19. Rees to Secretary, Archives of the Council for World Mission.

20. Patricia Frazer Lamb, "The Life and Writing of Mary Kingsley: Mirrors of the Self " (Ph.D. diss., Cornell University, 1977), p. 54.

21. Jane Moir, *A Lady's Letters from Central Africa* (Glasgow, 1891).

22. Mrs. Oliphant, "The Missionary Explorer," *Blackwood's Edinburgh Magazine* 83 (April 1858):386.

23. Alice Blanche Balfour, *Twelve Hundred Miles in a Waggon* (London, 1895).

24. Lucie Austin Duff Gordon, *Letters from the Cape* (London, 1864; rpt. 1875). All textual references are from the 1875 edition.

25. Lucie Austin Duff Gordon, *Letters from Egypt* (London: Routledge and Kegan Paul, 1969), p. 120.

Chapter Three

1. *Lady Florence Dixie in Glasgow* (Dundee: John Leng, 1891), p. 9.

2. Ibid.

3. Mary Wollstonecraft, *A Vindication,* p. 43.

4. George Bulwer Lytton, "To Little Florrie Douglas," in *Songs of a Child and Other Poems by "Darling"* (London, 1901–1902).

5. Ibid., p. 14.

6. Dixie to P. J. Smyth, September 10 (no year), Smyth Papers, National Library of Ireland. All letters to Smyth are from this collection.

7. Florence Dixie, *Abel Avenged: A Dramatic Tragedy* (London, 1877).

8. Caroline Douglas to P. J. Smyth, Smyth Papers.

9. Brian Roberts, *Ladies in the Veld* (London, 1965), p. 82.

10. Florence Dixie, "President Roosevelt's Gospel of Doom," *The Weekly Times and Echoes,* 18 April 1903.

11. Florence Dixie, *Isola; or the Disinherited: a revolt for woman and all the disinherited* (London, 1902), p. 7; hereafter page references cited in the text.

12. Florence Nightingale, *Cassandra* (Old Westbury, N.Y.: Feminist Press, 1979), p. 52.

13. Florence Dixie, *Across Patagonia* (London, 1880), p. 3; hereafter page references cited in the text.

14. Roberts, *Ladies in the Veld,* p. 84.

15. *The Life of Lady Florence Dixie,* a reprint from *The Leader,* n.d., p. 5.

16. Florence Dixie, *The Horrors of Sport* (London, 1895), p. 14.

17. Florence Dixie, *In the Land of Misfortune* (London, 1882), p. 1; hereafter cited in the text as *LM* followed by page number.

18. C. W. DeKiewet, *British Colonial Policy and the South African Republics, 1848–79* (London: Longmans, Green, 1929), p. 145.

19. Cecil Woodham-Smith, *Florence Nightingale* (New York: Mc-Graw-Hill, 1951), p. 55.

20. *London Figaro,* 8 February 1881, p. 4.

21. Wilson and Thompson, eds., *Oxford History of South Africa,* 2:265.

22. Bartle Frere to Michael Hicks Beach, 28 October 1879, in Donald Morris, *The Washing of the Spears* (New York: Simon and Schuster, 1965), p. 311.

23. *Morning Post* (London), 7 April 1881. Lady Dixie's despatches to the paper hereafter cited in the text as *MP* followed by date.

24. Anthony Trollope, *South Africa* (1878; rpt. Cape Town: A. A. Balkema, 1973), p. 369.

25. Roberts, *Ladies in the Veld*, p. 145.

26. H. Rider Haggard, *Cetewayo {sic} and His White Neighbours,* 2d ed. (London: Trubner, 1888), p. 13.

27. Hammond and Jablow, *Myth of Africa,* pp. 24–26.

28. Mrs. Wilkinson, *A Lady's Life and Travels in Zululand During Cetawao's {sic} Reign* (London: J. T. Hayes, 1882), p. 52.

29. Ibid., p. 129.

30. Haggard, *Cetewayo,* p. 2.

31. H. Rider Haggard, *King Solomon's Mines* (London and New York: Cassell, 1885), p. 234.

32. Norman A. Etherington, "Rider Haggard, Imperialism, and the Layered Personality," *Victorian Studies* 22 (Autumn 1978):71–87, points to this subconscious identification.

33. Roberts, *Ladies in the Veld,* p. 162.

34. Florence Dixie, "Cetshwayo and Zululand," *Nineteenth Century* 12 (August 1882):310.

35. Joyce Murray, ed., *Young Mrs. Murray Goes to Blomfontein, 1856–60* (Cape Town: A. A. Balkema, 1954), p. 13.

36. Louise Vescelles-Sheldon, *Yankee Girls in Zululand* (New York: Worthington, 1888), p. 59.

37. Mrs. Lionel Phillips, *Some South African Recollections* (London: Longmans, Green, 1899), p. 14.

38. Haggard, *Cetewayo,* p. 96.

39. Hammond and Jablow, *Myth of Africa,* p. 41.

40. Olive Schreiner, *The Story of an African Farm* (London: Chapman and Hall, 1883), p. 18.

41. *Athenaeum* (London), 25 November 1882, p. 691.

42. Ibid.

43. *Vanity Fair* (London), 25 November 1882, p. 313.

44. *The Life of Lady Florence Dixie,* p. 5.

45. Roberts, *Ladies in the Veld,* p. 90.

46. Ibid.

47. Dixie to William Gladstone, 23 October 1883, Gladstone Papers, British Library. All of Dixie's letters to Gladstone are from this collection.

48. Florence Dixie, "The Case of Ireland," *Vanity Fair* (London), 27 May 1882, p. 301.

49. *Vanity Fair* (London), 5 January 1884, p. 9.

50. *Vanity Fair* (London), 27 May 1882, p. 301.

51. Dixie to Gladstone, 29 November 1882, Gladstone Papers.

52. Ibid.

53. *Times* (London), 21 March 1883.

54. Elaine Showalter, *A Literature of Their Own* (Princeton: Princeton University Press, 1977), p. 186.

55. Florence Dixie, "Woman's Mission," *Vanity Fair* (London), 16 August 1884, pp. 114–15.

56. Dixie to Gladstone, 22 April 1892, Gladstone Papers.

57. Florence Dixie, *Redeemed in Blood* (London, 1889), p. 228; hereafter page references cited in the text.

58. Showalter, *A Literature of Their Own,* p. 182.

59. Florence Dixie, *Gloriana; or the Revolution of 1900* (London, 1890), p. 16.

60. Florence Dixie, "Woman's Mission," *Vanity Fair* (London), 16 August 1884, p. 115.

61. Showalter, *A Literature of Their Own,* p. 183.

62. Florence Dixie, *The Two Castaways; or Adventures in Patagonia* (New York, 1890), p. 8; hereafter page references cited in the text.

63. Florence Dixie, *Aniwee; or the Warrior Queen: A Tale of the Araucanian Indians* (London, 1890), p. 3; hereafter page references cited in the text.

64. Florence Dixie, "Memories of a Great Lone Land," *Westminster Review* (London) 139 (March 1893):247–56.

65. Florence Dixie, *Towards Freedom; an appeal to thoughtful men and women* (London, 1904), p. 50.

66. W. Stewart Ross, "A Daughter of the South: Lady Florence Dixie," *The Gallovidian* 7 (Winter 1905):200.

67. Ibid.

68. Florence Dixie, "Izra, or a Child of Solitude," *Agnostic Journal,* 31 December 1904, p. 228.

69. The former view is advanced by Morris, *Washing of the Spears,* p. 676; the latter by Roberts, *Ladies in the Veld,* pp. 1–6 and passim.

70. Ross, "A Daughter of the South," p. 200.

71. Caroline Douglas to P. J. Smyth, n.d., Smyth Papers.

Chapter Four

1. Mary Kingsley, "In the Days of My Youth: Chapters of an Autobiography," *M.A.P. (Mainly About People),* 20 May 1899, pp. 468–69; hereafter cited in the text as *M.A.P.* followed by page number.

2. I am indebted to Mrs. Dorothy Middleton for sharing this information with me.

3. George Kingsley, *Notes on Sport and Travel,* with a Memoir by his daughter Mary H. Kingsley (London, 1900), p. 9; hereafter cited in the text as *Notes* followed by page number.

4. Mary Kingsley to George Macmillan, 23 January 1898, Macmillan Papers, British Library. All textual references to Kingsley's letters to Macmillan are from this collection.

5. Ibid.

6. F. H. H. Guillemard to Stephen Gwynn, 21 November 1932, Gwynn Papers, National Library of Ireland.

7. Kingsley to Macmillan, 23 January 1898, Macmillan Papers.

8. Mary H. Kingsley, *West African Studies* (1899; 3rd ed. rev. London, 1964), p. 313; hereafter cited in the text as *WAS* followed by page number.

9. Guillemard to Gwynn, 21 November 1932, Gwynn Papers.

10. Ibid.

11. Lucy Toulmin-Smith, in Stephen Gwynn, *The Life of Mary Kingsley,* 2d ed. (London, 1933), p. 17; hereafter cited as Gwynn, *Life.*

12. Mary Kingsley to Alice Stopford Green, 27 January 1898, Alice Green Papers, National Library of Ireland. All textual references to Kingsley's letters to Green are from this collection.

13. Gwynn, *Life,* p. 17.

14. Mary Kingsley to Major Matthew Nathan, 12 March 1899, Nathan Papers, Bodleian Library, Oxford University. All textual references to Kingsley's letters to Major Nathan are from this collection.

15. Alice Green to John Holt, in Olwen Campbell, *Mary Kingsley: A Victorian in the Jungle* (London, 1957), p. 168.

16. Ibid.

17. Kingsley to Dennis Kemp, in Gwynn, *Life,* p. 153.

18. Kingsley to Matthew Nathan, 12 March 1899, Nathan Papers.

19. Gwynn, *Life,* p. 44.

20. Mrs. St. Loe Strachey, *St. Loe Strachey and His Paper* (London: V. Gollancz, 1900), p. 96. But Gwynn quotes Lady MacDonald as saying that Kingsley wore her brother's trousers while wading through swamps, *Life,* p. 267.

21. Mary H. Kingsley, *Travels in West Africa* (1897; 3rd ed. rev. London, 1965), p. 502; hereafter cited in the text as *TWA* followed by page number.

22. Mary Kingsley to Stephen Gwynn, 16 February 1899, Gwynn Papers, National Library of Ireland.

23. Ronald Robinson, John Gallagher, and Alice Denny, *Africa and the Victorians* (New York: St. Martin's Press, 1961), p. 14.

24. Kingsley to Matthew Nathan, 12 March 1899, Nathan Papers.

25. "The Lady-Errant," *Spectator* (London), 29 August 1891, pp. 285–87.

26. Cecil Howard, *Mary Kingsley* (London, 1957), p. 31.

27. Mary H. Kingsley, quoted in George A. Macmillan, Introductory Notice to Second Edition, *West African Studies* (3rd ed. rev. London, 1964), p. xxii.

28. Strachey, *St. Loe Strachey,* p. 96.

29. Kingsley to Macmillan, n.d., Macmillan Papers.

30. Kingsley to Dennis Kemp, in Gwynn, *Life,* p. 49.

31. Kingsley to Matthew Nathan, 27 January 1900, Nathan Papers.

32. Gwynn, *Life,* p. 49.

33. Kingsley to Macmillan, 14 August 1896, Macmillan Papers.

34. Gwynn, *Life,* p. 46.

35. Kingsley to John Holt, 14 November 1898, in Campbell, *Mary Kingsley: A Victorian in the Jungle,* p. 85.

36. Mary Slessor to Mr. Irvine, 12 December 1903, in Gwynn, *Life,* p. 278.

37. Mary H. Kingsley, "Travels on the Western Coast of Equatorial Africa," *The Scottish Geographical Magazine* 12 (1896):123.

38. Kingsley to Lady MacDonald, in Gwynn, *Life,* p. 131.

39. Kingsley to Macmillan, 21 November 1895, Macmillan Papers.

40. F.H.H. Guillemard to Kingsley, 1895, in Gwynn, *Life,* p. 45.

41. Gwynn, *Life,* p. 5.

42. Lord Palmerston in 1842, in Robinson, Gallagher, and Denny, *Africa and the Victorians,* p. 2.

43. Kingsley wrote approximately ninety letters to Macmillan between 1893 and her departure for South Africa in 1900. These are preserved in the Macmillan Papers, British Library. The letters cited in this paragraph are all from this collection.

44. The original copy of Kingsley's letter to Guillemard has not survived; however, she enclosed a copy of this letter in her correspondence with Macmillan, 20 August 1896, Macmillan Papers.

45. Kingsley to Dennis Kemp, in Gwynn, *Life,* p. 93.

46. Kingsley to Macmillan, n.d., Macmillan Papers.

47. Joseph Conrad, *The Heart of Darkness, Collected Edition of the Works of Joseph Conrad,* 21 Volumes (London: J. M. Dent, 1946–55), 16:62.

48. Margaret Atwood, *Survival, A Thematic Guide to Canadian Literature* (Toronto: Anans, 1972), p. 113.

49. Etherington, "Rider Haggard, Imperialism, and the Layered Personality," pp. 71–87.

50. Kingsley to Alfred Lyall, 5 May 1898, in Gwynn, *Life,* p. 146.

51. Kingsley to Macmillan, 8 May 1897, Macmillan Papers.

52. Patricia Frazer Lamb also makes this point in "The Life and Writing of Mary Kingsley: Mirrors of the Self " (Ph.D. diss., Cornell University, 1977).

53. Sylvan Barnet, Morton Berman, and William Burto, *A Dictionary of Literary, Dramatic, and Cinematic Terms* (Boston: Little, Brown and Co. 1971), p. 105.

54. MacLulich, "Canadian Exploration as Literature," p. 75.

55. Ibid.

56. Kingsley to Lady MacDonald, in Gwynn, *Life,* p. 131.

57. Ibid.

58. Kingsley to Macmillan, 20 August 1896, Macmillan Papers.

59. Gwynn, *Life,* p. 84.

60. Kingsley to Macmillan, 2 November 1896, Macmillan Papers.

61. Kingsley to Lady MacDonald, in Gwynn, *Life,* p. 131.

62. Guillemard to Gwynn, 21 November 1932, Gwynn Papers.

63. *Evening News* (London), 6 June 1900.

64. W. H. Auden, "Notes on the Comic," *The Dyer's Hand and Other Essays* (New York: Random House, 1962), p. 373.

65. Kingsley to Matthew Nathan, 3 October 1899, Nathan Papers.

66. Sheldon, *Sultan to Sultan,* p. 66.

67. Alice Stopford Green, "Mary Kingsley," *Journal of the African Society* 1 (October 1901):15.

68. Kinglsey to Macmillan, 24 March 1897, Macmillan Papers.

69. Mrs. George Macmillan related this unpublished story to Gwynn, who recorded it in his biography, *Life,* p. 93.

70. Rudyard Kipling, *Mary Kingsley* (Garden City, N.Y.: Doubleday, Doran and Co., 1932), pp. 2–3.

71. Macmillan's letter to Kingsley has been lost, but Kingsley's reply of 18 December 1894 states: "I do not understand quite what you mean by 'this story being told by a man.' " Macmillan Papers.

72. Robin Lakoff, *Language and Woman's Place* (New York: St. Martin's Press, 1969), p. 244.

73. *Concord,* April 1898, in Bernard Porter, *Critics of Empire: British Radical Attitudes to Colonialism in Africa, 1895–1914* (New York: St. Martin's Press, 1968), p. 244.

74. *Glasgow Herald,* 31 January 1899.

75. *Academy* (London), 9 June 1900.

76. Kingsley to Matthew Nathan, 28 August 1899, Nathan Papers.

77. Kingsley to Macmillan, 14 August 1899, Macmillan Papers.

78. Gwynn, *Life,* p. 225.

79. Gwynn, *Life,* p. 143.

80. Kingsley to Matthew Nathan, 8 March 1899, Nathan Papers.

81. Ibid.

82. Lamb, "Life and Writing of Mary Kingsley," p. 177.

83. *Athenaeum* (London), 6 February 1897.

84. *Athenaeum* (London), 27 February 1897.

85. *Daily Telegraph* (London), 13 November 1895, and Kingsley to John Holt, July 1899, in Campbell, *Mary Kingsley: A Victorian in the Jungle,* p. 151.

86. The original text of this speech was lost when the Society moved its headquarters. I am indebted here to Campbell, *Mary Kingsley: A Victorian in the Jungle,* pp. 151–52.

87. Kingsley to Mrs. Farquharson, 26 November 1899, Kingsley Papers, Royal Geographical Society.

88. Kingsley to Mr. Keltie, 1 January 1899, Kingsley Papers, Royal Geographical Society.

89. Kingsley to Matthew Nathan, 27 February 1900, Nathan Papers.

90. *The Cheltenham Ladies College Magazine* 38 (Autumn 1898), in Gwynn, *Life,* p. 103.

91. Kingsley to Macmillan, 18 December 1894, Macmillan Papers.

92. Kingsley to Gwynn, 16 February 1899, Gwynn, *Life,* p. 215.

93. *Spectator* (London), 6 March 1897.

94. *Athenaeum* (London), 6 February 1897.

95. Gwynn, *Life,* p. 24.

96. Ibid., p. 117.

97. Kingsley to Macmillan, 18 January 1897, Macmillan Papers.

98. Kingsley to Macmillan, 20 October 1897, Macmillan Papers.

99. Kingsley to John Holt, 29 November 1899, in Campbell, *Mary Kingsley: A Victorian in the Jungle,* pp. 153–54.

100. Kingsley to Macmillan, 4 December 1897, Macmillan Papers.

101. John E. Flint, "Mary Kingsley—A Reassessment," *Journal of the African Society* 4 (1963):103.

102. Robinson, Gallagher, and Denny, *Africa and the Victorians,* p. 398.

103. "The Transfer of the Niger Territories," *British Empire Review,* August 1899, p. 29.

104. Ibid., p. 504.

105. Sanche De Gramont, *The Strong Brown God* (Boston: Houghton Mifflin, 1976), p. 301.

106. Mary Kingsley, "The Position of Britain in the World," *Spectator,* 19 March 1899, pp. 407–8.

107. Kingsley to John Holt, April 1897, in Campbell, *Mary Kingsley: A Victorian in the Jungle,* p. 148.

108. Kingsley to Dennis Kemp, Gwynn, *Life,* p. 178.

109. Kingsley to Mr. Hartland, in Campbell, *Mary Kingsley: A Victorian in the Jungle,* p. 156.

110. Porter, *Critics of Empire,* p. 244.

111. Kingsley to Gwynn, 16 February 1899, in Gwynn, *Life,* p. 216.

112. Ibid.

113. Kingsley to E. D. Morel, February 1899, E. D. Morel Papers, Library, London School of Economics and Political Science. All letters to Morel are from this collection.

114. Kingsley to Matthew Nathan, 12 March 1899, Nathan Papers.

115. Kingsley to Dennis Kemp, 1898, in Gwynn, *Life,* p. 186.

116. Kingsley to Gwynn, August 1898, in Gwynn, *Life,* p. 191.

117. Mary H. Kingsley, *The Story of West Africa* (London, 1899), p. 19; hereafter cited in the text as *Story* followed by page number.

118. Kingsley to Matthew Nathan, 3 August 1899, Nathan Papers.

119. Gwynn, *Life,* p. 216.

120. Kingsley to John Holt, 1899, in Howard, *Mary Kingsley,* p. 216.

121. Kingsley to Matthew Nathan, 12 March 1899, Nathan Papers.

122. Gwynn, *Life,* p. 18.

123. Kingsley to Gwynn, n.d., Gwynn Papers, National Library of Ireland.

124. Kingsley to Matthew Nathan, 27 January 1900, Nathan Papers.

125. Kingsley to Matthew Nathan, 11 November 1899, Nathan Papers.

126. Kingsley to Matthew Nathan, 28 August 1899, Nathan Papers.

127. Gwynn, *Life,* p. 241.

128. Alice Green to John Holt, November 21, no year, in Lamb, "Life and Writing of Mary Kingsley," p. 197.

129. Gwynn, *Life,* p. 242.

130. Kingsley to Alice Green, 11 April 1900, Alice Green Papers, National Library of Ireland.

131. Gwynn, *Life,* p. 245.

132. Strachey, *St. Loe Strachey,* p. 99.

133. Gerald Carré, Chief Medical Officer, Simonstown Hospital, to Stephen Gwynn, 16 June 1900, Royal African Society.

134. Campbell, *Mary Kingsley: A Victorian in the Jungle,* p. 179.

135. Carré to Gwynn, 16 June 1900, Royal African Society.

136. Gwynn, *Life,* p. 254.

137. Campbell, *Mary Kingsley: A Victorian in the Jungle,* p. 179.

138. John E. Flint, Introduction to the Third Edition, *West African Studies* (1964), p. lxvi.

139. *Spectator,* 16 June 1900.

140. Green, "Mary Kingsley," p. 16.

141. John E. Flint, *Sir George Goldie and the Making of Nigeria* (London: Oxford University Press, 1960), p. 304.

142. John E. Flint, Introduction to the Third Edition, *West African Studies* (1964), p. xxxvi.

143. Gwynn, *Life,* p. 187.

Chapter Five

1. Susan Greenstein, "Sarah Lee, the Woman Traveller, and the Literature of Empire," *Design and Intent in African Literature,* ed. David Dorsey, Stephen Arnold, and Phanuel Egejuru (Washington, D.C.: Three Continents Press, 1981).

2. Ibid.

Selected Bibliography

PRIMARY SOURCES: LADY FLORENCE DIXIE

1. Travel and Political Books

Across Patagonia. London: Richard Bentley and Son, 1880.

A Defence of Zululand and Its King; echoes from the Blue Books. London: Chatto and Windus, 1882.

In the Land of Misfortune. London: Richard Bentley and Son, 1882.

2. Novels, Poems, and Plays

Abel Avenged: A Dramatic Tragedy. London: Edward Moxon, 1877.

Aniwee; or the Warrior Queen: a Tale of the Araucanian Indians. London: Henry and Co., 1890.

Gloriana; or the Revolution of 1900. London: Henry and Co., 1890.

Isola; or the Disinherited: a revolt for woman and all the disinherited. London: Leadenhall Press, 1902.

"Izra, or a Child of Solitude." *The Agnostic Journal,* January 1903–November 1905.

Redeemed in Blood. London: Henry and Co., 1889.

Songs of a Child and Other Poems by "Darling." London: Leadenhall Press, 1901–02.

The Story of Ijain, or the Evolution of a Mind. London: Leadenhall Press, 1903.

The Young Castaways, or the Child Hunters of Patagonia. London: J. F. Shaw, 1889. Published as *The Two Castaways; or Adventures in Patagonia.* New York: Dutton, 1890.

Waifs and Strays, or the Pilgrimage of a Bohemian Abroad. London: Griffith, 1884.

3. Articles and Pamphlets

"Affums: A True Story." *Vanity Fair,* 7 December 1881, pp. 4–6.

An Address to the Tenant Farmers and People of Ireland With Advice and Warning. Dublin: n.p., 1882.

"The Case of Ireland." *Vanity Fair,* 27 May 1882, p. 301.

"Cetshwayo and Zululand." *Nineteenth Century* 12 (August 1882):303–12.

The Horrors of Sport. Humanitarian League, Cruelties of Civilization, Vol. 2. London: William Reeves, 1895.

Ireland and Her Shadow. Dublin: Sealey, Bryers, and Walker, 1882.

"Memories of a Great Lone Land." *Westminster Review* 139 (March 1893):247–56.

"President Roosevelt's Gospel of Doom." *The Weekly Times and Echoes,* 18 April 1903.

"The True Science of Living." *Westminster Review* 150 (October 1898):463–70.

Towards freedom; an appeal to thoughtful men and women. London: Watts and Co., 1904.

"Woman's Mission." *Vanity Fair,* 16 August 1884, pp. 114–15.

Woman's Position, and the objects of the Women's Franchise League. Dundee: John Leng and Co., 1891.

4. Secondary Sources

Roberts, Brian. *Ladies in the Veld.* London: John Murray, 1965. An informal, unscholarly, and condescending biography of Florence Dixie and Theresa Longworth Yelverton.

PRIMARY SOURCES: MARY H. KINGSLEY

1. Books

Notes on Sport and Travel by George Kingsley. With a Memoir by his daughter Mary H. Kingsley. London: Macmillan and Co., 1900.

The Story of West Africa. London: Horace Marshall, 1900.

Travels in West Africa. London: Macmillan and Co., 1897; 3rd ed. rev. London: Frank Cass and Co., 1965.

West African Studies. London: Macmillan and Co., 1899; 3rd ed. rev. London: Frank Cass and Co., 1964.

2. Articles

"African Religion and Law." *National Review* 29 (September 1897):122–39.

"Administration of our West African Colonies." *Monthly Record,* Manchester Chamber of Commerce, 30 March 1899.

"Black Ghosts." *Cornhill,* July 1896, pp. 79–92.

"The Development of Dodos." *National Review* 27 (March 1896):66–79.

"The Fetish View of the Human Soul." *Folklore* 8 (June 1897):138.

"Fishing in West Africa." *National Review* 29 (May 1897):213–27.

"The Forms of Apparitions in West Africa." *Journal of the Psychical Research Society* 14 (July 1899).

"The Hut Tax in Africa." *Spectator,* 19 March 1898, pp. 407–8.

"The Law and Nature of Property among the Peoples of the True Negro Stock." *Proceedings,* British Association, September 1898.

"A Lecture on West Africa." *Cheltenham Ladies' College Magazine* 38 (Autumn 1898).

"The Liquor Traffic with West Africa." *Fortnightly Review* 69 (April 1898):537–60.

"The Native Populations of Africa." *Spectator,* 15 May 1897, pp. 695–96.

"A Parrot Story." *Cornhill,* September 1897, pp. 389–91.

"The Position of Britain in the World," *Spectator,* 19 March 1898, pp. 407–8.

"The Throne of Thunder." *National Review* 27 (May 1896):357–74.

"The Transfer of the Niger Territories." *British Empire Review,* August 1899, pp. 29–31.

"Travels on the Western Coast of Equatorial Africa." *Scottish Geographical Magazine* 12 (1896):113–24.

"Two African Days' Entertainment." *Cornhill,* March 1897, pp. 354–59.

"West Africa from an Ethnological Point of View." *Imperial Institute Journal,* April 1900.

3. Secondary Sources

Blyden, Edward M. "The African Society and Miss Mary Kingsley." London: J. Scott and Co., 1900. A reprint of a series of articles from the *Sierra Leone Weekly* which quotes several Kingsley letters about West Africa and describes the formation of the African Society in her honor.

Campbell, Olwen. *Mary Kingsley: A Victorian in the Jungle.* London: Methuen, 1957. A biography which uses material that Gwynn omitted and tries to offer psychological insight into the effect of Kingsley's childhood on her character.

Clair, Colin. *Mary Kingsley: African Explorer.* Figures of the Commonwealth Series. Watford, Herts.: Bruce and Gawthorn, 1963. A biographical rehash of well-known facts.

Flint, J. E. "Mary Kingsley—A Reassessment." *Journal of African History* 4 (1963):95–104. An analysis of Mary Kingsley's political stance which argues that she is above all the spokeswoman for the interests of the British traders.

Green, Alice Stopford. "Mary Kingsley." *Journal of the African Society* 1 (October 1901):1–16. A loving memoir by a close friend which discusses Kingsley's achievements and their emotional price.

Glynn, Rosemary. *Mary Kingsley in Africa.* London: George Harrop, 1956. A chatty, novelistic biography with some errors of fact.

Gwynn, Stephen. *The Life of Mary Kingsley.* 2d ed. London: Macmillan and Co., 1933. The indispensable, although badly documented, biography written by a friend and employing private letters from Kingsley.

Hughes, Jean. *Invicible Miss; the Adventures of Mary Kingsley.* London: Macmillan and Co., 1968. An uninspired biography.

Howard, Cecil. *Mary Kingsley.* London: Hutchinson, 1957. A breezy, unscholarly biography with some factual inaccuracies.

Kipling, Rudyard. *Mary Kingsley.* Garden City, N.Y.: Doubleday, Doran and Co., 1932. A memoir based on a few meetings which celebrates her courage.

Wallace, Kathleen. *This is Your Home; A Portrait of Mary Kingsley.* London: Heinemann, 1956. A simply written, unscholarly re-telling of her life.

PRIMARY SOURCES: WOMEN TRAVELLERS

Baker, Anne, ed. *Morning Star: Florence Baker's Diary of the expedition to put down the slave trade on the Nile, 1870–73.* London: William Kimber, 1972.

Balfour, Alice Blanche. *Twelve Hundred Miles in a Waggon.* London: Edward Arnold, 1895.

Barkly, Fanny. *Among Boers and Basutos.* London: Remington and Co., 1893.

Broome, Mary Anne Barker (Lady M. A. Barker). *A Year's Housekeeping in South Africa.* London: Macmillan and Co., 1877.

Duff Gordon, Lucie Austin. "Letters from the Cape," *Vacation Tourists and Notes of Travel in 1862–63.* Edited by Francis Galton. London: 1864. Reprinted in *Last Letters from Egypt to which are added Letters from the Cape.* London: Macmillan and Co., 1875.

Hore, Annie B. *To Lake Tanganyika in a Bath Chair.* London: Sampson, Low, Marston, Searle, and Rivington, 1886.

Hutchinson, Louisa. *In Tents in the Transvaal.* London: Richard Bentley and Son, 1879.

A Lady [Elizabeth Melville]. *A Residence at Sierra Leone.* Edited by Hon. Mrs. Norton. 1849. Reprint. London: Frank Cass and Co., 1968.

Moir, Jane. *A Lady's Letters from Central Africa.* Glasgow: James Maclehose and Sons, 1891.

Petherick, Mr. and Mrs. *Travels in Central Africa and Explorations of the Western Nile Tributaries.* 2 vols. London: Tinsley Brothers, 1869.

Pringle, M. A. *Towards the Mountains of the Moon: A Journey in East Africa.* London and Edinburgh: W. Blackwood and Sons, 1884.

Ward, Harriet. *Five Years in Kaffirland.* 2 vols. London: Henry Colburn, 1848.

Index

DATE DUE
